ON THE ART OF
CROSS-EXAMINATION

Four Great Old Authorities,

Two Englishmen and Two Americans,

with Emphasis on Their Principles

GEORGE A. SERGHIDES

Ph.D. (*Exon*, U.K.), Ph.D. (Athens, Gr.), Ph.D. (Salonica, Gr.),
President of the Family Court of Nicosia-Kyrenia (Cyprus), International
Hague Network Judge, Adjunct Law Professor at the University of Cyprus,
Editor of and main Author of "*Studia Juriis Cypri*"

ON THE ART OF
CROSS-EXAMINATION

Four Great Old Authorities,

Two Englishmen and Two Americans,

with Emphasis on Their Principles

With a Foreword by
DEMETRIOS H. HADJIHAMBIS

LL.B. *Exon*, Ph.D. *Cantab.*
Judge of the Supreme Court of Cyprus
Formerly Lecturer-in-Law at the University of Exeter

The Lawbook Exchange, Ltd.
Clark, NJ

EDITOR'S NOTE

This book reveals the wisdom of four nineteenth century eminent English and American lawyers, Cox, Ballantine, Brown and Hardwicke, on the art of cross-examination of witnesses, by classifying and discussing their principles on the topic.

Copyright © 2009 G.A. Serghides
Lawbook Exchange paperback edition 2013
ISBN 978-1-61619-350-8

THE LAWBOOK EXCHANGE, LTD.

33 Terminal Avenue
Clark, New Jersey 07066-1321

Please see our website for a selection of our other publications and fine facsimile reprints of classic works of legal history:
www.lawbookexchange.com

Library of Congress Cataloging-in-Publication Data

Serghides, George A.
   On the art of cross-examination : four great old authorities, two Englishmen and two Americans with emphasis on their principles / by Dr. G.A. Serghides; With a Foreword by Dr. Demetrios H. Hadjihambis. -- Lawbook Exchange paperback edition.
      pages cm
   Includes bibliographical references.
   ISBN 978-1-61619-350-8 (pbk. : alk. paper) -- ISBN 1-61619-350-6 (pbk. : alk. paper)
   1. Cross-examination--United States. 2. Trial practice--United States. 3. Cross-examination--England. 4. Trial practice--England. 5. Cox, Edward W. (Edward William), 1809-1879 6. Ballantine, William, 1812-1887. 7. Brown, David Paul, 1795-1872. 8. Hardwicke, Henry, 1861-1909 I. Title.
   K5460.S47 2013
   347'.075--dc23   2013005435

Printed in the United States of America on acid-free paper

IN MEMORIAM TO

MY FATHER

ANDREAS G. SERGHIDES
(1923-1996)
of Gray's Inn, Barrister

ACKNOWLEDGEMENTS

It is my duty first to express my gratitude to Dr. Demetrios H. Hadjihambis for the foreword.

My grateful thanks are due also to Mr. Jack Gaist for the proofreading of this book.

Finally, I thank my mother Loukia (classical musician), my wife Dora (advocate) and my daughter Arsenia for their continuous emotional support.

CONTENTS

FOREWORD

Reading through this new treatise of Dr. Serghides when he kindly asked me to foreword it, I found myself all the more drawn into and fascinated by what he aptly terms in the title as the art of cross-examination; and finally came to form the conviction that this was largely due to the excellent choice of his sources and authorities, the four nineteenth century eminent English and American masters of advocacy, Cox, Ballantine, Brown and Hardwicke.

Through them, what in the book emerge as principles and rules of cross-examination are to be understood not as mere statements of theoretical import and remoteness but as living truth drawn from experience and the understanding of human nature. Their statement and discussion then becomes not a dry process unrelated from a concrete context but a gratifying and absorbing journey into the infinite parameters of a matter that forms the very essence of the judicial operation—the establishment of disputed truth in human relations. As the book proceeds, the long-established and perfected principles and rules of cross-examination unfold with logical consistency and interrelation and are illustrated by simple and practical references, reminding us that what was obtained in older times is still as valid and relevant today.

For the elements of which the art of cross-examination is moulded are constant—knowledge of the facts and the law, understanding of human nature, wisdom, common sense and, above all, a gentlemanly approach to the high duty of the advocate not as a mercenary to his client´s interests set at destroying hostile evidence but as his representative in the truth-finding exercise. To these, of course, must be added another element which, of its nature, cannot be discussed and analysed but is nevertheless essential in distinguishing the par excellence cross-examiner – talent, equated to the Socratic "mania," so elusive to define and yet so obvious when revealed.

Dr. Demetrios H. Hadjihambis
Judge of the Supreme Court of Cyprus

INTRODUCTION

THE FOUR AUTHORITIES

In this book, I classify and discuss the principles of cross-examination employed by four great old authorities, two Englishmen and two Americans, thus:

THE ENGLISHMEN

Edward William Cox (1809-1879), Serjeant-at-Law, *The Advocate, his Training, Practice, Rights and Duties,* vol. I., London, 1852,[1] chapter XXXIV on cross-examination, pp. 375-434. This is the only edition and there is no other

---

[1] Cox was a prolific writer. He wrote a lot of studies on psychology. (See p. 28, n. 21 below).   He is also famous of this works: *The Principles of Punishment as Applied in the Administration of Criminal Law, by Judges and Magistrates*, London, 1877, reprint New York 1984; *The Arts of Writing, Reading and Speaking in letters to a law student*, London, 1863, New York 1870 and many other editions and reprints; *Reports of Cases in Criminal Law Argued and Determined in all the Courts in England and Ireland*, London, 1846. *Vide* also Peter Spiller, *Cox and Crime: An Examination of Edward William Cox, his Career and his Approach to the Criminal Law of his Time*, Cambridge, 1985.

volume published by the author under the same title. This is a very rare book.

William Ballantine (1812-1887), Serjeant-at-Law, *Some Experiences of a Barrister's Life,* vol. I, London, 1882,[2] chapter X, pp. 123-130. This book consists of two volumes and, since 1882 when it was first published, there have been many editions, the latest in 2008. The substance of all the editions is the same.

---

[2] See also of the same: *The Old World and the New*, London, 1884.

THE AMERICANS

David Paul Brown (1795-1872), member of the Philadelphia Bar, *The Forum; or Forty Years Full Practice at the Philadelphia Bar,* vol. I., Philadelphia, 1856,[3] section on cross-examination (in his "Bibliographical Memoir"), pp. lxxvii-lxxx. This book consists of two volumes and, since 1856 when it was first published, there have been many impressions, the latest in 2007. The substance of all the impressions is the same.

---

[3] See also *The Forensic Speeches of David Paul Brown*, selected from important trials and embracing a period of forty years, edited by Robert Eden Brown, Philadelphia, 1873.

Copies of Hardwicke's *Art of Winning Cases*
from my personal law library

Henry Hardwicke (1861-1909), member of the New York Bar, *The Art of Winning Cases or Modern Advocacy – A practical treatise on preparation for trial, and the conduct of cases in court,* New York and Albany, 1894,[4] chapter IV on cross-examination, pp. 138-237. There was a second impression of the book in 1899 and a second edition in 1903 as well as a new impression of the second edition in 1922. The substance of the two editions and all the impressions is the same.

As is clear, Cox's and Hardwicke's chapters on examination are longer than Ballantine's and Brown's relevant text. However, all four authorities are of equal significance.

---

[4] See also by the same author: *History of Oratory and Orators*, New York – London, 1896; *The Trial Lawyer's Assistant in Civil Cases*, Albany, 1902; *The Art of Rising in the World*, New York, 1896; *The Art of Getting Rich*, New York, 1897; *The Art of Living Long and Happily*, London, 1895.

From tens of books on advocacy and cross-examination contained in my private library, these four books have most greatly impressed me. The contribution of all four authorities on the issue of cross-examination is great though not unique because, as explained in another book,[5] most of the principles of cross-examination were employed first by Socrates, Aristotle, Cicero and Quintilian. And it is so not only because their text is marvellous, clear and unambiguous, but also because their principles are based on the wisdom, experience and common sense of their authors. The importance of Cox's, Ballantine's and Brown's rules is admitted by Hardwicke who in his own text cites all the relevant texts of the previous three authors.[6] As regards the works of Brown and Cox, Hardwicke says that he knows of no more valuable rules of cross-examination of a witness than those laid down by the two authors and he considers Cox's book, which is not to be found easily, admirable. He then gives their rules in full. As regards Ballantine's observations, which he also gives in full, he says that they may prove instructive to his readers.

The rules of Cox, Ballantine and Brown, apart from all being cited by Hardwicke, have also in common the fact that they are all cited by another great authority on the examination of witnesses, Sir Frederic John Wrottesley,[7]

---

[5] *The Technique of Cross-Examination, The Golden Rules of Cross-Examination and Four Masters of Antiquity, Two Greek (Socrates and Aristotle) and two Latin (Cicero and Quintilian)*, Nicosia, 2007 (*Studies in Cyprus Law,* vol. 7, study 6) (in Greek).
[6] Without referring to the relevant pages, Hardwicke refers pp. 157-160 to Ballantine's rules (pp. 123-129), pp. 184-187 to Brown's rules ((lxxvii-lxxx) and pp. 187-233 to Cox's rules (pp. 375-434).
[7] *The Examination of Witnesses in Court, Founded on "the Art of Winning Cases by Henry Hardwicke and "The Advocate" by Edward W. Cox,* 3rd edn., London, 1961.

who, citing almost all the text of Hardwicke,[8] unavoidably includes all the previous three authorities.[9]

Another great authority on examination of witnesses, James Ram, in an Appendix to his book,[10] includes Cox's and Brown's rules of cross-examination, the title page informing readers that this is so.

As all four authorities have more general titles, one would not be in the position to know that they deal also with cross-examination of witnesses without further study of them.

My humble contribution to their work is to make known and classify their principles so that they may be more easily read and remembered. There is a lot of citation of the text of the authorities in order for the reader to know the actual words used by them. It is to be noted that all four authorities are more than one hundred years old.

---

[8] Pages 58-133 of Wrottesley where Hardwicke is cited (pp. 187-233). However, in these pages no mention is made in Hardwicke though this citation is clear from page v of Wrottesley, "preface to first edition" where it is said that the author takes liberties with the text of Hardwicke. This is clear also from the title of Wrottesley's book (see n. 7 above) as well as from the comparison of the text of Wrottesley to that of Hardwicke. It is worthy of mention that Wrottesley in certain points rewrites Hardwicke's text on the rules of evidence so as to include the current law of his time. The rest of Hardwicke's text is intact apart from the omission of the reference to Harris (pp. 165-172 of Hardwicke) and the inclusion of a reference to Sir Frank Lockword (Wrottesley, pp. 81-83).
[9] Pages 91, 93-130 include Cox (375-434), pages 74-76 include Ballantine (pp. 123-129), and pages 91-93 include Brown (pp. lxxvii-lxxx).
[10] *A Treatise on Facts as Subjects of Inquiry by a Jury*, New York, 1873, reprint Colorado, 1982. In pages 324-360, James contains Cox's rules (pp. 375-433) and in pages 321-322, he contains Brown's rules (pp. lxxvii-lxxx).

CROSS-EXAMINATION–
THE SEVEREST TEST OF AN ADVOCATE'S SKILL

Hardwicke remarks[11] that the origin of correct cross-examination is lost in the dim mists of antiquity, but that it is of ancient origin there can be no doubt.[12] Solomon, as he notices, seems to have favoured it as a means of establishing truth for he says "He that is first in his own cause, seemeth just, *but his neighbor cometh and searcheth him.*"

In my view the best thesis on the difficulty and importance of cross-examination is given by Cox.

Cox begins the chapter on cross-examination of his admirable book by saying that cross-examination "is commonly esteemed <u>the severest test of an Advocate's skill</u>, and perhaps it demands, beyond any other of his duties, the exercise of his *ingenuity.*"[13]

And he well elaborates on his thesis, thus:

> It is undoubtedly a great *intellectual effort*; it is the direct conflict of mind with mind; it demands, not merely much knowledge of the human mind, its faculties and their *modus operandi*, to be learned only by reading, reflection and observation, but much experience of man and his motives, as derived from intercourse with various classes of many persons, and, above all, by that practical experience in the art of dealing with witnesses

---

[11] *The Art of Winning Cases or Modern Advocacy,* New York and Albany, 1894, 184.
[12] *See G. A. Serghides, The Technique of Cross-Examination, the Golden Rules of Cross-Examination and Four Masters of Antiquity, Two Greek (Socrates and Aristotle) and two Latin (Cicero and Quintilian),* Nicosia, 2007, vol. 7 of *Studies in Cyprus Law.*
[13] *The Advocate, His Training, Practice, Rights, and Duties,* vol. I., London, 1852, 374. My underlining.

which is more worth than all other knowledge; which other knowledge will materially assist, but without which no amount of study will suffice to accomplish an Advocate. To the onlooker, a cross-examination has much more interest, for it is more in the nature of a combat with the excitement that always attends a combat of any kind, physical or intellectual; it is a man against a man, mind wrestling with mind. [14]

On the importance of cross-examination as the only agent by which falsehood is exposed Ballantine says the following:

The records of courts of justice from all time show that truth cannot in a great number of cases tried be reasonably expected. Even when witnesses are honest, and have no intention to deceive, there is a natural tendency to exaggerate the facts favourable to the cause for which they are appearing, and to ignore the opposite circumstances: and the only means known to English law by which testimony can be sifted is cross-examination. By this agent, if skillfully used, falsehood ought to be exposed, and exaggerated statements reduced to their true dimensions. [15]

Ballantine also observes that cross-examination is the only means by which perjury can be exposed. [16]

STRUCTURE

From the relevant text of the four authorities I endeavoured to trace the most important principles which are classified

---

[14] *Op. cit.* 375-376.
[15] *Some Experiences of a Barrister's Life,* vol. I., London, 1882, 123-124.
[16] *Op. cit.* 130.

according to their nature. Due to their general application, the first seventeen principles are examined separately while other principles and many trial tactics are examined under the general sub-headings "first object, second object and third object of cross-examination and tactics", because they are more connected to the particular purpose of cross-examination.

RULES OF EVIDENCE

Principle #1

THE CROSS-EXAMINER MUST HAVE A GOOD KNOWLEDGE OF RULES OF EVIDENCE

Cox in his chapter "professional studies"[1] says this on the importance of the law of evidence for the lawyer.

> Next in natural sequence to the *Practice of the Courts* and *Pleading* comes the *Law of Evidence*, to the Advocate the most indispensable of all branches of legal knowledge, and which he needs to possess, not merely *stored* in the memory, but so *arranged* there that it can be produced in a moment, when occasion requires. For, be it observed, the application of the Law of Evidence almost always occurs in the course of a trial, when there is no time for reference and very little for reflection; when an objection, if not taken on the instant, before the words are out of the witness's mouth, comes too late, and which, if taken, must be supported with reasons which there will be no leisure to make search after in books; they must be at the tongue's tip, ready for instant use. Undoubtedly this promptitude of application can only be acquired by practice; the most accomplished lawyer is perplexed at first; but the knowledge itself must be obtained in the study, by reading, – the manner of its employment is the education of the *Court.*

Elsewhere in the same chapter Cox says very instructively for lawyers:

> The *Law of Evidence* being of such primary importance to the Advocate, it should be read with particular attention to the system of noting previously recommended. And when the book preferred has been completed, it should not be laid aside altogether, but thenceforward, mingled with the studies of each day, should be the *re-perusal* of some portions of the Law of Evidence, or of the leading cases by

---

[1] *The Advocate, His Training, Practice, Rights and Duties,* London, 1852, 144-145. My underline but not my italics.

which its most important principles, or their exceptions, have been established.[2]

Hardwicke begins his chapter[3] on cross-examination by giving a few of the leading principles of the law of evidence which should govern counsel in the conduct of the cross-examination. He emphasizes that "[c]ross-examination undoubtedly affords the best security against incomplete, distorted, or false evidence...."[4]

What these rules are depends on the law of each country. The cross-examiner must be aware of the most recent rules of evidence law which apply in his country. The rules to which Hardwicke refers are rules of common law which still apply in common law countries.

These rules according to Hardwicke are the following, the numbering of which, however, is mine:

1. "[I]n putting questions upon cross-examination, much greater latitude is allowed than upon examination-in-chief.[5] Especially is this true where the object of the questions asked is to affect the credit of the witness and questions of this kind have been allowed where they affected the character of the witness, and consequently his credit, although such questions had no relation to matter in issue."[6]

2. "A witness ... cannot be cross-examined as to any facts which, if admitted, would be collateral and wholly irrelevant to matters in issue, and which could in no matter affect his credit."[7]

---

[2] *Op. cit.* 146. My underlining but not my italics.
[3] *The Art of Winning Cases or Modern Advocacy*, chapter IV, p. 138.
[4] *Op. cit.* 139.
[5] See also *op. cit.* 179.
[6] *Ibid.* In p. 179 he says that "a witness may not be cross-examined as to collateral and irrelevant matters merely for the purpose of afterward contradicting or impeaching him."
[7] *Ibid.*

3. "Witnesses upon cross-examination may be asked as to any vindictive or revengeful expression they may have used against any party to the cause, where such expressions would affect the credit or the character of the witness. But the answers of witnesses to irrelevant questions cannot, as a general rule, be contradicted; consequently, if the party choose to cross-examine a witness as to an irrelevant and collateral fact, he is bound by the answer of the witness."[8]

4. *Former contradictory accounts.* A witness may be asked if upon some former occasion a different and contradictory account of the same subject was given.

If he gives an affirmative answer, the question affects his credit no matter whether the subject of the answer be relevant to the issues involved.[9]

On the other hand, if he answers in the negative and the subject of the answer be *irrelevant* to the issues concerned, the answer is conclusive and the witness cannot be contradicted by other witnesses. However, if the answer be *relevant* to the issues, then evidence may be given "to show that on the former occasion the witness has given a different account of the same matter and the inquiry is made for the purpose of laying a foundation for proof of contradictory statements."[10]

5. *Kinds of former contradictory statements.* These statements may be of two kinds, *verbal* and *in writing.*[11]

6. *Verbal statements.* In such case the witness must be asked "all the particulars of the supposed contradictions which are to be afterwards brought forward against him, before any contradiction is attempted" "[H]e must be also

---

[8] *Op. cit.* 138-139.
[9] *Op. cit.* 139.
[10] *Ibid.*
[11] *Ibid.*

asked as to the *time, place* and *person involved* in the supposed contradiction."[12]

And he goes on to explain which is the foundation of this rule: "[t]he reason of this rule is found *in justice,* and is intended to protect the witness, for as the direct tendency of the evidence is to impeach *his veracity,* by showing that he has made a contradictory statement to some one else, justice requires that before his credit is attacked, he should have an opportunity to state whether he made such statement to that person...." "It is a matter of common knowledge that it is very easy to be mistaken as to what was said in conversation. It may have been only partially heard, or partially forgotten, and besides it may have been falsely reported...."[13]

On the matter in issue, Hardwicke says that it is a matter of some doubt whether a verbal statement of the character we have mentioned before, can be proved *where a witness has been asked about it and he neither admits nor denies it.* He also states[14] that there are two views on the topic and refers to the relevant common law authorities which are cited below.

In *Crowley v. Page,*[15] Parke, B., admitting the evidence, said the following:

> Evidence of statements of witnesses on other occasions relevant to the matter in issue, and inconsistent with the evidence given by them on the trial, is always admissible, in order to impeach the value of their testimony; but only such statements as are relevant are admissible, and in order to lay foundation for the admission of such contradictory statements and to enable the witness to explain them (and, as I conceive, for that purpose only), the witness may be asked whether he ever said what is suggested to him with

---

[12] *Ibid.* The emphasis is mine.
[13] *Ibid.* The emphasis is mine.
[14] *Op. cit.* 140-141.
[15] 7 C. & P. 791.

the name of the person to whom, or in whose presence he is supposed to have said it, or some other circumstances sufficient to designate the particular occasion. If the witness, on the cross-examination, admits the conversation imputed to him, there is no necessity for giving further evidence of it; but if he says he does not recollect, that is not an admission, and you may give evidence on the other side that the witness did say what is imputed,- always supposing the statement to be relevant to the matter at issue. This has always been my practice. If the rule were not so, you could never contradict a witness who said he could not remember.

A different view, however, was taken in *Pain v. Beeston*,[16] and in *Lord v. Hitchcock*.[17] In the former case, Tindal, C.J., clearly said that he had never heard such evidence admitted in contradiction, except where the witness had expressly denied the statement and he rejected the evidence.

Hardwicke says that he is inclined to believe that the ruling of Parke, B., is more in accordance with the dictates of common-sense and more in harmony with adjudications in analogous cases than those of the Judges in the other two cases. I also adhere to this view because, as Hardwicke goes on to say, "if the rule were otherwise, a witness under the pretence of *not remembering* might make a false statement, knowing it to have been false, and still escape exposure and contradiction."[18]

---

[16] 1 Mo. & R. 20.
[17] 9 C. & P. 619 (*per* Lord Abinger).
[18] *Op. cit.* 141. The emphasis belongs to Hardwicke.

ENGLISH CURRENT RULES

There are five exceptions to the rule that, if a witness is cross-examined as to facts not material to the issue between the parties, his answer must be taken, and may not be contradicted:

(a) if a witness denies that he has been convicted of a criminal offence, evidence may be adduced to prove that he was so convicted;
(b) evidence may be adduced to show that a witness has a bias or partiality against a party to the case;
(c) evidence may be adduced of the reputation of a witness for untruthfulness;
(d) medical evidence may be adduced to show that a witness is unreliable;"
(e) evidence may be adduced to challenge the credibility of the maker of an admissible hearsay statement, such evidence being akin to that which might have been adduced if the maker of the statement had been called to give evidence.[19]

As Murphy says,

[a]t common law, it was open to a cross-examiner to ask a witness about any previous inconsistent statements he may have made, but the rule was circumscribed by the requirements that, if the statement put was in writing, the witness must be shown the document before he could be asked whether he had said something different on another occasion (which removed the element of surprise); and that if the statement was proved, having been denied by the witness, it must be made evidence as part of the cross-examiner's case (which inhibited the use of statements in many cases). The use of previous inconsistent statements

---

[19] Murphy *on Evidence,* 10th edn., Oxford, 2008, 574. See also analysis on pp. 574-580.

in cross-examination is now governed by s. 4 and s. 5 of the Criminal Procedure Act 1865.[20]

Under section 4,

If a witness, upon cross-examination as to former statement made by him relative to the subject-matter of the indictment or proceeding, and inconsistent with his present testimony, does not distinctly admit that he has made such statement, proof may be given that he did in fact make it; but before such proof can be given, the circumstances of the supposed statement, sufficient to designate the particular occasion, must be mentioned to the witness and the he must be asked whether or not he has made such statement.

According to Murphy,

[t]he section is not expressed to apply exclusively to oral or written statements, and it may be assumed that s.4 is intended to apply to both written and oral statements. It is implicit in the section that the cross-examiner is entitled to ask the witness about the former statement, and the draftsman evidently considered that he was building upon that rule of common law. The right to prove the making of any statement which is not 'distinctly admitted' covers both outright denials and ambivalent or evasive answers as to whether the witness made the previous statement. It also precludes the objection that the proof of the previous statement, if denied, might offend against the rule of common law that answers in cross-examination which go only to collateral matters must be accepted as final.

The section applies alike to statements made previously on oath, for example, a deposition made in committal proceedings, and those made previously

---

[20] *Op. cit.* 570.

unsworn in any circumstances, for example on being interviewed by the police.[21]

The general application of s. 4 was emphasised in *R. v. O' Neill*.[22] There, M and O were tried together, M having pleaded guilty to the first of the two counts in the indictment, to which O had pleaded guilty. M gave evidence on his own behalf and in cross-examination was asked whether O had committed with him the offence alleged in count one. Upon M denying O's involvement, M's verbal statement to the police in which he said the opposite was put to him under s. 4. The Court of Appeal held that such a course was proper as was the exercise of the judge's discretion in allowing it.

Under section 5,

A witness may be cross-examined as to previous statements made by him in writing or reduced into writing, relative to the subject-matter of the indictment or proceeding, without such writing being shown to him; but if it is intended to contradict such witness by the writing, his attention must, before such contradictory proof can be given, be called to those parts of the writing which are to be used for the purpose of contradicting him: Provided always, that is shall be competent for the judge, at any time during the trial, to require the production of the writing for his inspection, and he may thereupon make such use of it for the purposes of the trial as he may think fit.

Wrottesley says,

[t]hus, to take a concrete instance, you may, as counsel, be in possession of a letter, written by the witness, in which he has made a statement at variance with his present

---

[21] *Op. cit.* 570.
[22] [1969] Crim.LR. 260. See also Phipson *on Evidence,* 14th edn., London, 1990, p. 256, § 12-24.

testimony. But the statement, though in this one particular in your favour, may be otherwise extremely hostile to your case. And you would thus be confined to such use of the letter as you could make of it, without having to put the whole letter in evidence.

In this case, you would ask the witness whether he wrote such a letter, and then handing it to him, and allowing him to read it to himself, you would ask him *not* whether he had written something there which did not tally with his present testimony, but whether, having read the letter, he persisted in that statement made in his testimony that day.

And in the case of an honest witness, the result might very well be that he would qualify that statement in your favour.

And your opponent would not by this means become entitled to see the document you were using, *nor* to re-examine upon it,[23] though of course he may re-examine upon the subject-matter of your questions.[24]

Murphy also says,

[i]f the answer is that the witness is prepared to alter his evidence materially, the damage to his credit is done. If he sticks to his evidence, the cross-examiner must choose

---

[23] On the contrary, Phipson *on Evidence,* 15th edn., London, 2000, on p. 256, § 11-29, says: "Two comments can be made on these rules. First, it must permissible for re-examination to introduce sufficient parts of the statement to correct any misleading impression created by the selection of the extracts relied on in cross-examination. Secondly, the restrictions on re-examination are perhaps in any event due for reconsideration: if a small part of statement is used to show inconsistency, it is difficult to see the logic for preventing the introduction of the remainder of the statement, subject to discretionary exclusion, to demonstrate the extent to which the witness has in fact been inconsistent."
Phipson's view who follows the commentary of Professor D. Birch on *R. v. P. (GR),* [1998] Crim.L.R. 663, 664-5, seems to be just for the witness but in my view is not so in line with the purpose of the section.
[24] *The Examination of Witnesses in Court,* 3rd edn., London, 1961, 63.

whether to accept that answer, or whether to enter the second stage. If he chooses the latter course, he will proceed to contradict the witness by the document, in other words put to him that it is the document (identifying it to him) that is a true account, rather than the witness's evidence. At this point, but not before - another significant departure from the common law rule - the document may be proved to contradict the witness, and must then be put in evidence, having of course been made relevant by the second stage of cross-examination.

As to the evidential value of previous inconsistent statements, Murphy summarizes as follows:

> At common law, where a previous inconsistent statement was used for the purpose of cross-examination as to credit, it was evidence only of the inconsistency of the witness, and was not admissible as evidence of any matters stated. Statute has now altered this rule, both in civil and criminal cases.... In civil cases, s. 6(3) of the Civil Evidence Act 1995 preserves the circumstances under which a statement may become evidence by virtue of s. 4 or s. 5 of the Criminal Procedure Act 1865, but where the statement becomes evidence, it is now admissible as evidence of the matters stated as well as of inconsistency by virtue of s. 1 and s. 6(1) of the Act. Section 119(1) of the Criminal Justice Act 2003 has the same effect in criminal cases.[25]

Remember

• *The rules of evidence must be on the tip of the cross-examiner's tongue.*

---

[25] *Op. cit.* 571.

LEGAL AND GENERAL KNOWLEDGE

Principle #2

THE CROSS-EXAMINER MUST HAVE A
THOROUGH KNOWLEDGE OF THE
SUB-STANTIVE LAW AND THE RULES OF COURT.
HE MUST ALSO HAVE A GENERAL KNOWLEDGE
OF A WIDE RANGE OF SUBJECTS.

THE MOST IMPORTANT OF THE ADVOCATE'S
MENTAL QUALIFATIONS IS PERCEPTION.

Cox, in a chapter of his book under the title "capacities", says that the advocate "cannot be wise on one subject alone".[1] He continues thus:

> His intellect must not be cultivated in parts. His information must be universal as the range of human inquiry. His intelligence must have no limits but those of the human mind. All learning of the past that is contained in books, and of the present as it moves before his eyes, the philosophy of the study and the business of actual life, must be familiar to him – not, indeed, with the perfect mastery of a professor, for that is as unnecessary as impossible, but with such general knowledge of the facts of science and art, and of the processes by which they are pursued, as may enable him to deal with matters not foreign to his thoughts, and to talk of them in such manner as may be easily intelligible to the unlearned, and yet shall not subject him to the ridicule of the scientific. He needs equally large learning and vigorous common sense; imagination to give a glow to eloquence; strong emotions wherewithal to persuade, and power of argument by which to convince… For him there is not time for previous 'cramming;' he must possess this various knowledge beforehand, and so that it may be ready for use at any moment.[2]

Cox says that the advocate must study treatises on various branches of substantive law[3] and books of practice[4] including rules of procedure[5] and rules of evidence.[6] On the last topic we have already provided a separate chapter.

---

[1] *The Advocate, His Training, Practice, Rights and Duties,* London, 1852, 6.
[2] *Op. cit.* 6-7.
[3] *Op. cit.* 134.
[4] *Ibid.*
[5] *Op. cit.* 136.
[6] *Op. cit.* 144-145.

Elsewhere Cox says that the advocate must study, *inter alia,* classics,[7] mathematics, geometry, physiology, anatomy, physical science, acoustics, optics, history, rhetoric, grammar, logic, religion, languages, fine arts,[8] psychology,[9] economics,[10] poetry,[11] chemistry,[12] mechanics,[13] geography,[14] physical science,[15] and moral, ethical,[16] political,[17] mental[18] and spiritual[19] philosophy.

Cox had shown particular interest in psychology. His study *Psychology of Memory and Recollection,*[20] is very useful for advocates conducting cross-examination.[21]

---

[7] *Op. cit.* 49.
[8] *Op. cit.* 97.
[9] *Op. cit.* 108-109.
[10] *Op. cit.* 116.
[11] *Op. cit.* 124.
[12] *Op. cit.* 100
[13] *Op. cit.* 101
[14] *Op. cit.* 96.
[15] *Op. cit.* 95-96.
[16] *Op. cit.* 97 and 110.
[17] *Op. cit.* 97, 105 and 110.
[18] *Op. cit.* 97 and 105.
[19] *Op. cit.* 105.
[20] Psychological Society of Great Britain, Paper 9, London, 1876.
[21] Some other of his studies in psychology are the following: *Has a Man a Soul*, Psychological Society of Great Britain, Paper 15, London, 1877; *The Mechanism of Man: An Answer to the Question What Am I*, a popular introduction to mental physiology and psychology, 3r edn., London, 1879; *On Some of the Phenomena of Sleep and Dream*, Psychological Society of Great Britain, Paper 2, London, 1875; *Progress and Prospects of Psychology*, Psychological Society of Great Britain, Paper 10, London, 1878; *The Province of Psychology*, Psychological Society of Great Britain, Paper 1, London, 1875; *Psychology Proved by Physical Science*, Psychological Society of Great Britain, Paper 12, London, 1877; *Spiritualism Answered by Science*, London, 1871.
Perhaps Cox's particular interest in psychology was due to the fact that his son, W. S. Cox, died from fever in 1897, after taking up missionary

According to Cox, the most important of the advocate's mental qualifications is PERCEPTION, i.e. keenness of observation, clearness and quickness of comprehension.[22] Needless to say this qualification is very important for conducting a successful cross-examination. A prerequisite of it is, in my view, general knowledge.

Remember

- *The cross-examiner must have a thorough knowledge of the substantive law and the rules of court.*
- *He must also have a general knowledge of a wide range of subjects.*
- *The most important of the advocate's mental qualifications is perception.*

---

work in Sierra Leone. See E. W. Cox, *Early Promoted – a Memoir of W. S. Cox,* London, 1897.

[22] *Op. cit.* 14-18.

FACTS

FACTS

FACTS

Principle #3

**THE CROSS-EXAMINER MUST KNOW
THE FACTS OF THE CASE WELL**

Ballantine supports the view[1] that, in order to attain success in cross-examination, it is necessary for counsel to form in his own mind an opinion upon the facts of the case.

Cox emphasizes that it is upon the facts as stated by the client that legal advice is given and the case is dealt with in court.[2]

Similarly, Hardwicke notes that "[t]o be thorough in the preparation of the law and facts in every case, is one rule that the advocate cannot safely violate".[3]

Brown, describing himself in his "Biographical Memoir", says: "... he rarely resorts to notes, either for evidence or arrangement; but having, as it were, *everything in his own mind,* his great effort seems to be to transfuse it into the minds of others."[4]

Remember

- *The cross-examiner must know the facts of the case well.*

---

[1] *Some Experiences of a Barrister's Life,* vol. I, 1882, 124.

[2] *The Advocate, His Training, Practice Rights and Duties*, vol.I, London, 1852, ch. xxix "Advising on Evidence", 312, ch. xxx "Reading a Brief", 313.

[3] *The Art of Winning Cases or Modern Advocacy,* New York and Albany, 1894, ch. 1 "Preparation for Trial", 5.

[4] *The Forum; Forty Years Full Practice at the Philadelphia Bar,* vol. I, cxx-cxxi. My emphasis.

CHARACTER AND MOTIVES

Principle #4

THE CROSS-EXAMINER MUST FORM IN HIS MIND AN OPINION UPON THE CHARACTER AND PROBABLE MOTIVES OF A WITNESS

Ballantine asserts[1] that, in order to attain success in cross-examination, it is necessary for counsel to form in his own mind an opinion upon the character and probable motives of a witness before asking a question.

As he explains, "[t]his doubtless, requires experience; and the success of his cross-examination must depend upon the accuracy of the judgment he forms."[2]

Cox as will be seen makes the course which might be adopted in cross-examination dependent on the character of the witness.[3]

Remember

• *The cross-examiner must form in his mind an opinion upon the character and probable motives of a witness, before asking a question.*

---

[1] *Some Experiences of a Barrister's Life,* vol. I, 1882, 124.
[2] *Op. cit.* 124-125.
[3] See pp. 139-141 *post.*

BODY LANGUAGE

Principle #5

**THE CROSS-EXAMINER MUST NEITHER
TAKE HIS EYE FROM THAT OF THE WITNESS
NOR BE REGARDLESS OF HIS VOICE**

Brown's first two[1] out of his nine rules of cross-examination deal with body language.

The first rule is that, save in indifferent matters, cross-examining counsel must never take his eye from that of the witness. He rightly observes that "this is the channel of communication, from mind to mind, the loss of which nothing can compensate." And he goes on to say this in inverted commas:

> Truth, falsehood, hatred, anger, scorn, despair,
> And all the passions – all the soul is there.

Brown's second rule of cross-examination it that the cross-examiner must not be regardless of the voice of the witness since "next to the eye, this is perhaps the best interpreter of his mind". "The very design to screen conscience from crime, the mental reservation of the witness, is often manifested in the tone or accent, or emphasis of the voice."

Brown gives an excellent instance where the cross-examiner must be watchful of the voice of a witness who tries to evade.

Suppose that it is important to know that the witness was at the corner of Sixth and Chestnut streets at a certain time. He is asked at his cross-examination: "Were you at the corner of Sixth and Chestnuts streets at six o' clock? If the witness was sincere his answer would perhaps be "I was near there". But if he is not frank and he is desirous to conceal a fact and defeat the object of the inquiry,[2] his answer would perhaps be that "I was not at the *corner* at *six* o' clock" although he may have been very close to that place. As Brown well remarks "[e]mphasis upon both words[3] plainly implies a mental

---

[1] *The Forum; Forty Years Full Practice at the Philadelphia Bar,* vol. I, 1856, 124-125.

[2] Speaking to the letter rather than to the spirit of the inquiry.

[3] Thus upon *"corner"* and *"six"*.

evasion or equivocation, and gives rise, with a skillful examiner to the question, At what hour were you at the corner? or at what place were you at six o' clock? And in nine instances out of ten, it will appear that that the witness was at the place about the time, or at the time about the place."

Cox says that it is wrong to suppose that when a witness dispenses with questions and pours out his whole story in a continuous stream, he is therefore always lying.[4] The advocate's care will be to distinguish between the witness who runs through his story telling the truth and the one who is merely repeating a lesson learned by heart (taught testimony).[5] As he observes, "close observation" will enable him "to discover a difference in the look, the tone, the manner and the language".[6] Again, therefore, BODY LANGUAGE is important. Cox starts with body language for recognizing that a witness is not lying.

He says that:

> Close observation will enable you to discover a difference in the look, the tone, the manner and the language. When relating what he has *seen*, there is always an aspect of intelligence, even in the dullest; the eye kindles, the face brightens, the expression changes with the incidents narrated. Still more does the *tone of the voice* reveal the speaker's truth; its changes are dramatic; it varies with every emotion that flashes across the mind, awakened by the recalling of the incidents described. The *manner* is usually eager and energetic and in strict accordance with the tones, the aspect, and the theme. And even if these signs should be wanting you must not, therefore, decide against the veracity of the witness, until you have considered his *language*. If he is honest, his

---

[4] *The Advocate, His Training, Practice, Rights and Duties,* vol. 1, 1852, 417.
[5] *Op. cit.* 418.
[6]*Ibid.* My underline.

language will always <u>be such as is consistent with his
condition of life – appropriate to age, sex, education and
calling.</u> Moreover, it will exhibit that fitness for the
subject, without reference to structure of sentences, which
always distinguishes extempore narrative. If these
characteristics, or either of them, be present, you may
safely assume that the witness is telling the truth, but that
he is only able to do so after his own fashion of a
continuous story, and cannot recall it by scraps, under
interrogation.[7]

If, on the other hand, as Cox continues, the witness is
repeating by rote a lesson which he has committed to
memory, the advocate will find wanting in him all or most of
the signs of truth above described. He further explains thus:

> <u>He stands quite still</u>, excepting, it may be, <u>an uneasy
> motion of the hands or feet. His face has no meaning in it.
> His eyes are fixed, not upon the Counsel, the Judge, or the
> Jury, but upon the wall, or more commonly turned
> upwards, with a sort of vacant stare. His voice is
> monotonous and expresses no emotion. His delivery is
> rapid,</u> unless when seized by a sudden forgetfulness, when
> he makes a full stop, or, after stumbling a little, tries back
> again, in hope to regain the lost word or thought. <u>His
> language, also, is almost always *in*appropriate to his
> position, for in such case it would seldom be his own
> composition that he has learned, but something which
> another has put into words, and which words would not be
> those of the pupil, but of the master. A single expression</u>
> will often suffice to betray to you this sort of *taught
> testimony*, when it is one which you know that such a
> person as the witness would not have used, and perhaps

---

[7] *Op. cit.* 418-419. My underlining.

there is no test so difficult to evade, and so conclusive where it prevails, as this of *language*.[8]

Cox advises that if the advocate asks the witness to repeat his account of the transaction, he will do so in almost the selfsame words, with the same aspect and manner, and in the same tone, differing palpably from his bearing and <u>tone and language before and after the episode</u>.[9] Here again body language is important.

Cox also in many other parts of his famous treatise on cross-examination refers to the importance of the art of reading the mind of the witness in his face (i.e. his countenance, the tone of his voice, the language he utters, etc.)[10]

According to Cox, as will be seen later,[11] a witness who is lying will not look the advocate boldly and fully in the face with a steady gaze. His eye quivers and turns away. On the contrary the truthful witness will meet the advocate's gaze and will let the advocate look into his eyes.

Hardwicke's comments on body language will be instructive:

> The eye, the tones of the voice and the mouth are the best indexes to the state of mind of witness. A convulsive twitching of the muscles of the mouth will often betray

---

[8] The reason for this as he says is plain: "A witness learns his lesson thus. He tells what he knows to the Attorney, or this Clerk. If they be of the unscrupulous class, which has happily become so rare, the witness is informed that his evidence is of no use, but that if he had known so and so he would have been taken to the Assizes. The hint suffices. The memory is racked again, and the testimony desired is then found. It is taken down in writing. His entire story is put into formal shape; it is read over to him again and again, until he has it almost by heart. He learns, not merely *the facts* he is to prove, but the very *words* in which those facts are narrated in the brief, and he repeats them as he has learned them." (p. 420).

[9] *Op. cit.* 420.

[10] See pp. 140, 164 *post.*

[11] See p. 141 *post.*

agitation which the witness wishes to conceal.....But the advocate should never take his eye from the face of a witness, for if he is seen at an unguarded moment the expression of his eye or the movement of the muscles of the mouth will reveal the ruling sentiment of his mind. For cross-examination may be regarded as a MENTAL DUEL between witness and advocate, and it has been said that 'the advocate, who takes his eyes from the witness is as likely to be worsted as the swordsman who lets his eyes wander from his adversary.'[12]

Subsequently, Hardwicke says that for unnumbered ages external appearance has been deemed to be an index to the internal man and in the Gentoo Code we find the following curious passage:[13]

When two persons upon a quarrel refer to arbitrators, those arbitrators at the time of examination shall observe both the plaintiff and the defendant narrowly, and take notice if either, and which of them, when he is speaking, hath his voice falter in his throat, or his colour change, or his forehead sweat, or the hair of his body stand erect, or a trembling come over his limbs, or his eyes water, or if, during the trial, he cannot stand still in his place, or frequently licks and moistens his tongue, or hath his face grow dry, or in speaking to one point wavers and shuffles off to another, or, if any person puts a question to him, is unable to return an answer; from the circumstances of such commotions, they shall distinguish the guilty party.

---

[12] *The Art of Winning Cases or Modern Advocacy,* New York and Albany, 1894, 153.
[13] *Op. cit.* 153-154. Hardwicke does not make any reference to the relevant pages of the Gentoo Code. However the right reference is this *A Code of Gentoo Laws or Ordinations of the Pundits from a Persian Translation made from the original, written in the shanscrit language, London,* M.DCC.LXXVII, chap. III, sect. VI, 106-106.

Hardwicke later on says that: "[t]he signs of guilt spoken of, however, are not always infallible, for innocent persons when unjustly accused of crime are often so deeply mortified that they look as if they were guilty".[14]

On the same lines with Hardwicke, Ballantine alleges that "[e]mbarrassment exhibited under a searching cross-examination is not to be relied on as a proof of falsehood; the novelty of the position or constitutional nervousness may frequently occasion it."[15] He then gives a remarkable instance of this in a trial in which he was engaged to defend the prisoner:

> It was a curious case. Messrs. Coutts, the bankers, were in the habit at certain periods of remitting specie to a bank at Oxford by a coach that went to that city. The money was contained in a box, and placed under the charge of a coachman. Upon a particular day, when the supposed box arrived at its destination, it was found to contain rubbish, the real one having been subtracted. It was proved that my client, who was a passenger, had got down before the end of the journey, with no apparent excuse, and did not take his seat again. Beyond this, however, there was little to sustain the charge against him. The coachman naturally was a principal witness, but became so embarrassed, and answered questions in so shuffling a manner, although with perfect truth, that both the judge and jury believed that he was an accomplice in the robbery, and in this opinion I confess I shared.
>
> My client was acquitted, but shortly afterwards was tried and convicted of another offence. I took the opportunity (I think, through the medium of the chaplain) to ask how the Oxford robbery had been effected, and learnt that the coachman had, against orders, gone into a public-house to get a glass of ale, and it was during his

---

[14] *Op. cit.* 154.
[15] *Some Experiences of a Barrister's Life,* vol. I., London, 1882, 127.

absence that the prisoner contrived to convey the dummy to an accomplice in front, receiving from him the genuine box, with which he decamped.[16]

Remember

- *The cross-examiner must be watchful of the eyes and the voice of the witness.*
- *A witness who is lying will not look the advocate boldly and fully in the face with a steady gaze. His eye quivers and turns away. The truthful witness will on the contrary meet the advocate's gaze and will let the advocate look into his eyes.*
- *The embarrassment of a witness is not a sign of his falsehood.*

---

[16] *Op. cit.* 128-129.

PLAIN AND SIMPLE QUESTIONS

Principle #6

THE CROSS-EXAMINER MUST FRAME HIS QUESTIONS IN PLAIN AND SIMPLE LANGUAGE

Hardwicke says[1] that "it is highly important, in cross-examination, for the advocate to frame his questions in plain, simple language, adapted to the understanding of the witness." He also says that it often occurs that the witness during his cross-examination does not understand the questions of the cross-examiner and the cross-examiner does not understand the answers of the witness. Witnesses feel more at home when questioned in plain and simple language, and the jury as well as court and counsel will understand what is said.[2]

Furthermore he states that a provincial pronunciation of words is a source of mistakes of this kind.[3]

Hardwicke to make his point even more clear, apart from giving some examples, refers[4] to the following words of Wesley[5] to one of his law-assistants:

> Clearness is necessary for you and me, because we are to instruct people of the lowest understanding; therefore, we, above all, if we *think* with the wise, must yet *speak* with the vulgar. We constantly use the most common, little, easy words (so they are pure and proper) which our language affords. When first I talked at Oxford to plain people in the castle and the town, I observed they gaped and stared. This quickly obliged me to alter my style, and adopt the language of those I spoke to.

Hardwicke emphasizes that the great lawyers Rufus Choate and Daniel Webster were partial to plain, simple words and that many of the advocates of his time who use words of "learned length and thundering sound" in their

---

[1] *The Art of Winning Cases or Modern Advocacy*, 143.
[2] *Op. cit.* 146.
[3] *Op. cit.* 144.
[4] *Ibid.*
[5] John Wesley (1703-1791) was an Anglican minister and Christian theologian who was an early leader in the Methodist movement.

questions to witnesses would do well to adopt the style of these great masters of the art of advocacy.[6]

Remember

• *The cross-examiner must frame his questions in plain, simple language, adapted to the understanding of the witness.*
• *The greatest lawyers were partial to plain, simple words.*

---

[6] *Op. cit.* 145-146.

BE BRIEF

Principle #7

THE CROSS-EXAMINER MUST BE BRIEF

Ballantine understands the advantage for the advocate being brief in his cross-examination. For this reason he refers to Sir William Follett and says this:

"The object of cross-examination is not to produce startling effects, but to elicit facts which will support the theory intended to be put forward. Sir William Follett asked the fewest questions of any counsel I ever knew; and I have heard many cross-examinations from others listened to with rapture by an admiring client, each question of which has been destruction to his case."[1]

Similarly, Hardwicke says that a prudent advocate will ask as few questions as possible.[2]

It is true that the length of the question usually determines the length of the answer. So the witness is under control when the questions are short and especially leading.

Remember

• *The cross-examiner must be brief.*

---

[1] *Some Experiences of a Barrister's Life,* vol. I., London, 1882, 125.
[2] *The Art of Winning Cases or Modern Advocacy,* New York and Albany, 1894, 153.

ONE QUESTION TOO MANY

Principle #8

**WHEN THE CROSS-EXAMINER HAS OBTAINED
EVERYTHING POSSIBLY HELPFUL
FROM THE WITNESS
HE MUST THEN STOP AND KEEP HIS SEAT**

The difficulty for the cross-examiner is recognizing the one question too many. As soon as the advocate asks the question, he will recognize it. He must be able to know when he has obtained everything possibly helpful from the witness and then stop and take his seat.

Cox at the end of his chapter on cross-examination says the following on the topic:

> There are no harmless questions here; the most apparently unimportant may bring destruction or victory. <u>If the summit of the *orator's* art has been rightly defined to consist in knowing *when to sit down,* that of *an Advocate* may be described as knowing when *to keep his seat*.</u> Very little experience in our courts will teach you this lesson, for every day will show to your observant eye instances of self-destruction brought about by imprudent cross-examinations. Fear not that your discreet reserve will be mistaken for carelessness or want of self-reliance. The true motive will soon be seen and approved. Your critics are Lawyers who know well the value of discretion in an Advocate, and how indiscretion in cross-examination cannot be compensated by any amount of ability in other duties. The Attorneys are sure to discover the prudence that governs your tongue. Even if the wisdom of your abstinence be not apparent at the moment, it will be recognized in the result. Your fame may be of slower growth than that of the talker, but it will be larger and more enduring. The issue of a case rarely depends upon a speech, and is but seldom even affected by it; *but there is never a cause contested the result of which is not mainly dependent upon the skill with which the Advocate conducts his cross-examination.*[1]

Brown, stating his fourth principle of cross-examination, says this on the point under discussion:

---

[1] *The Advocate, His Training, Practice, Rights, and Duties,* vol. I, London, 1852, 433-444. My underline but not my italics.

In a criminal, especially in a capital case, so long as your cause stands well, ask but few questions, and be certain NEVER TO ASK ANY, THE ANSWER TO WHICH (IF AGAINST YOU,) MAY DESTROY YOUR CLIENT, unless you know the witness perfectly well, and know that his answer will be favorable equally well; or unless you be prepared with testimony to destroy him, if he play traitor to the truth and your expectations.[2]

Ballantine, on the same lines, say this:

And it ought, above all things, to be remembered by the advocate, that when he has succeeded in making a point, HE SHOULD LEAVE IT ALONE until his turn comes to address the jury upon it. If a dishonest witness has inadvertently made an admission injurious to himself, and, by the counsel's dwelling upon it, becomes aware of the effect, he will endeavour to shuffle out of it and perhaps succeed in doing so.[3]

Ballantine in another place in his treatise remarks thus:

...and unless counsel is able to arrive in his own mind at a satisfactory opinion it is far better to ask nothing than to flounder on with the chance of getting out something by a crowd of questions.[4]

---

[2] *The Forum; or Forty Years Full Practice at the Philadelphia Bar,* vol. I, Philadelphia, 1856, lxxviii- lxxix. My emphasis.
[3] *Some Experiences of a Barrister's Life,* vol. I, London, 1882, 125.
[4] *Op. cit.* 126.

Remember

• When the cross-examiner has obtained everything possible helpful from the witness he must then stop and keep his seat.

• He must never ask any question the answer to which may destroy his client.

REPETITION OF QUESTIONS

Principle #9

**REPETITION OF QUESTIONS IS GENERALLY
DISAPPROVED BY JUDGES.
HOWEVER, IF THE CROSS-EXAMINER USES THIS
METHOD TO DETECT FALSITY, HE CAN INSIST
KINDLY AND FIRMLY, SHOWING TO THE COURT
THAT HIS CROSS-EXAMINATION IS NOT
PURPOSE-LESS.**

On the repetition of questions Cox makes the following very instructive points:

> We have already noticed the difficulty sometimes experienced by an Advocate, and especially by the beginner, from the impatience of the Judge at repetitions of the same questions. Too often he is met with the remark, 'Mr. ...., you have asked that question before,' or 'The witness has already told you.' This is doubly disagreeable, for besides putting you on ill terms with the Court, it disturbs your plans, and sets the witness on his guard. There is nothing of which the Bench is so little tolerant as of the repetition of the same questions, and yet there are few more effective methods of detecting a falsehood. The witness answers. You note his answer. You pass away to some distant part of the story, or some foreign transaction. You then suddenly return, when his thoughts have been otherwise engaged, when probably he has forgotten his first answer, if it was false, and you obtain a different one, which instantly betrays him. Often have we seen witnesses, who were proof against all other tests, fail before this one. When your design is distinctly this, and not merely a vague, purposeless interrogation, proceed respectfully, but firmly, to show that you have a meaning, and your aims will soon come to be understood and respected by the Court.[1]

Remember

- *The cross-examiner should avoid repeating a question unless he uses this as a means for detecting falsity, in which case he must persist until he achieves his purpose.*

---

[1] *The Advocate, His Training, Practice, Rights and Duties,* vol. I, London, 1852, 410-411.

ADJURATIONS TO WITNESSES

Principle #10

**THE CROSS-EXAMINER SHOULD NOT INDULGE
TOO MUCH IN ADJURATIONS TO WITNESSES
TO SPEAK THE TRUTH, REMINDING THEM
CONTINUOUSLY THAT THEY ARE ON THEIR OATH**

Cox's very useful advice is that the advocate <u>should not indulge too much in adjurations to witnesses to speak the truth, reminding them continuously that they are on their oath</u>, as "Now, sir, upon your solemn oath"; "Remember you are upon your oath, and take care what you say;" and the like.[1] Cox then goes on to say:

> If frequently introduced, they lose their force by repetition. They are very effective when judiciously employed and uttered with due solemnity of tone and manner, and *on fit occasions;* but they should not be put forward on every slight pretence, to frighten an honest, as to awe a dishonest, witness. Reserve such an appeal for times when it may be used with effect, because with obvious propriety. When you believe that a witness is tampering with his conscience, you may sometimes successfully prevent the contemplated perjury by a solemn appeal, and especially if you add to it an exhortation not to be hasty, but to think before he speaks. The countenance, the tone of the voice, the very attitude, should express the language you utter. You may word it somewhat after this fashion, 'Remember, you may have sworn to tell the truth, and the whole truth. Now'. – (put the question, and add) – 'think before you speak, and answer me truly as you have called God to witness your words.'[2]

Similarly, Hardwicke referring, to a writer of experience, states thus:

> 'It is common practice to tell a witness over and over again to mind he is upon his oath. Few witnesses bear this repeated admonition patiently. But when used in moderation, and free from angry tone, the witness has no reason to

---

[1] *The Advocate, His Training, Practice, Rights and Duties,* vol. I, London, 1852, 412.
[2] *Op. cit.* 412-413.

complain of it, for it is known that some persons will *say* that they will not *swear.*"[3]

Remember

• *The cross-examiner should not indulge too much in adjurations to witnesses to speak the truth. Moderation should be employed.*

---

[3] *The Art of Winning Cases or Modern Advocacy,* New York-Albany, 1894, 146.

BE WISE

Principles #11, 12 & 13

**#11 THE CROSS-EXAMINER MUST ASK ONLY
QUESTIONS TO WHICH HE ALREADY
KNOWS THE ANSWERS.**

**#12 HE SHOULD NEVER PERMIT A WITNESS
TO GIVE REASONS FOR HIS BELIEF.**

**#13 HE SHOULD NOT PERMIT A WITNESS
TO SIMPLY REPEAT WHAT HE SAID
ON DIRECT EXAMINATION.**

Hardwicke[1] deals with the above three principles by referring to a very instructive example given by Harris,[2] including Harris' very useful comments. Let us consider this example.

We will suppose a man to be charged with having, years ago, at a country fair, bought a horse and paid for it with a bad cheque.

The case is simple enough, and the defence will be of course that the prisoner is not the man.

Certain facts are necessary to be brought out in cross-examination to establish the defence, because counsel for the prosecution, knowing the baldness of his own case, has stated it with great caution and called exactly enough evidence to convict, if left alone by defendant's counsel.

Then Harris gives an example[3] of bad cross-examination in the case under discussion and later on an example of good cross-examination. Both cross-examinations are of course as to the identity of the prisoner.

He starts with a bad cross-examination where all of the first three above principles are violated:

1. *Q,*- 'Had you ever seen the man who bought your horse before?'
    A.- 'No.'
2. 'How long were you with him?'
    - 'Several hours.'
3. Were other people present?'
    - 'Yes, a great many.'
4. 'When did you next see the man after that day?'
    -'Not until I saw him at the police station.'
5. 'Did you know him at once, or pick him out?'
    - 'I knew him directly.'
6. 'How did you know him?'

---

[1] *The Art of Winning Cases or Modern Advocacy,* New York and Albany, 1894, 165-170.
[2] *Illustrations in Advocacy,* 5th edn., London, 1915, 79-83.
[3] *Op. cit.* 80-82.

- 'From his appearance.'
7. 'And you undertake to swear on your solemn oath he is the man?'
- 'Undoubtedly.'

Hardwicke agrees with Harris that with these questions the prisoner must be convicted for the following reasons:

The *first* question is right because defending counsel <u>knows what the answer will be and must elicit it before the jury</u>. It is one point in his favour.

The *second* question is wrong because, in the first place, <u>he does not know what the answer will be,</u> and secondly the witness will understand from its form how to make his reply as telling as he can against the prisoner.

The *third* question is also wrong in form because it gives the prosecutor at once the clue to its meaning: <u>it therefore endangers its meaning</u>. The question should be put in a less direct form, <u>for fear the answer would be against the prisoner</u>.

The principle deriving from these three questions therefore is that THE CROSS-EXAMINER MUST ASK ONLY QUESTIONS TO WHICH HE ALREADY KNOWS THE ANSWER.

The *fourth* question was right, no other answer in the circumstances being possible. And besides because it fixed a vast space of time between the day of the fair and the police court.

The *fifth* question was wrong because in the form in which it was put it could not be answered in the prisoner's favour.

The *sixth* question was wrong because it gave the witness the opportunity of giving reasons for his belief, making his belief look like a fact. No witness will give a reason that is in favour of the cross-examiner.

The principle deriving from the sixth question is that THE CROSS-EXAMINER SHOULD NEVER PERMIT A WITNESS TO GIVE REASONS FOR HIS BELIEF.

The *seventh* question was also wrong for every reason. It was a repetition of what the prosecutor had said in his examination-in-chief. As Harris says, it was not a cross-examination at all and could only confirm the evidence already given. And again, it was only asking the witness whether he would "undertake" to do what he had already done.

The principle deriving from the seventh question is that THE CROSS-EXAMINER SHOULD NOT PERMIT A WITNESS TO SIMPLY REPEAT WHAT HE SAID ON DIRECT EXAMINATION.

All these three principles according to my view are based on logic and common sense and this is why I classify them under the general principle "Be Wise".

Hardwicke remarks that similar to the above bad questions are put over and over again, even by leaders, without any definite calculation of their value or any knowledge of their practical effect.[4]

Now let us see another style of cross-examination to the same witness suggested by Harris[5] as a good example and by which of course the witness must be acquitted.

Question No. 1 will stand as above.

Instead of question No. 2, the cross-examiner asks where the witness saw the prisoner. This may save the trouble of putting the third question. He will get the answer that he was at the fair, and most likely in a public-house, full of all kinds of people, blacklegs and others.

The question "What time was it?" will now safely follow. The witness, knowing nothing of his object, gives the true time probably, let us say "about twelve o' clock".

---

[4] *Op. cit.* 165.
[5] *Op. cit.* 83.

The next question will separate them in a few minutes, instead of leaving them together for several hours (which could not be true).

The farmers' ordinary was at half-past twelve, and the prisoner was gone before that.

The next answer will show that from the time he parted with him, after the cheque was given, he never saw him again until he picked him out at the police station.

A clever question or two as to the dress of the man, or the colour of his neck-cloth, stand-up or turndown collar, will confound the witness, and, if he has not great patience, he must lose his temper, and probably ask how he can be expected to recollect all this after such a distance of time.

A last question or two about the man's whiskers, whether he had any or not, will make him feel, as Harris says,[6] that he would rather be at a horse fair than in a witness-box.

Cox alleges that it is a waste of time for the cross-examiner and helps the witness more than himself to repeat the selfsame questions his advocate asks him during examination-in-chief. The reason for this is obvious as the witness is well prepared for these questions and therefore will repeat the lesson he has learned without alteration or hesitation.[7] This practice is the almost universal fault of beginners and inexperienced advocates. Cox describes it as follows:

> With a slight alteration of phrase and an attempt to be stern in tone and eye, they persist in repeating the very question which the witness has already distinctly answered. 'Do you mean to tell the Jury upon your oath that you heard him say so?' 'Will you swear you saw Smith strike him?' and such like; to which the answer is 'I

---

[6] *Op. cit.* 83.
[7] *The Advocate, His Training Practice, Rights and Duties,* vol. I, London, 1852, 428.

have said so already.' 'I *have* sworn it." No other answer could be expected. The witness had come prepared to prove these very facts .... This manner of proceeding is, therefore, WORSE THAN WORTHLESS.[8]

Remember

- *The cross-examiner must be wise.*
- *He must ask only questions to which he already knows the answers.*
- *He should never permit a witness to give reasons for his belief.*
- *He should not permit a witness to simply repeat what he said on direct examination.*

---

[8] *Op. cit.* 428-429. My capitals but not by italics.

BE ALWAYS WATCHFUL

Principle #14

THE CROSS-EXAMINER MUST ALWAYS BE WATCHFUL.

HE SHOULD BE AWARE OF THE DANGER OF THE CROSS-EXAMINATION BEING TOO MINUTE AND CIRCUMSTANTIAL.

HE SHOULD BE AWARE OF THE FACT THAT THROUGH A SMALL OPENING IN CROSS-EXAMINATION A RE-EXAMINATION ON THE SAME POINT MAY BE ADMITTED.

The cross-examiner must always be watchful. Brown likens a cross-examiner to a skilful chess-player. He states, as his seventh and eighth principles of cross-examination the following:

> Like a skilful chess-player, in every move FIX YOUR MIND UPON THE COMBINATIONS AND RELATIONS OF THE GAME – partial or temporary success may otherwise end in total remediless defeat.[1]

> NEVER UNDERVALUE YOUR ADVERSARY; BUT STAND STEADILY UPON YOUR GUARD. A random blow may be just as fatal, as though it were directed by the most consummate skill – the negligence of one often cures, and sometimes renders effective, the blunders of another.[2]

Hardwicke,[3] gives an illustration to explain the principle that the cross-examiner must be watchful.

The illustration concerns a case where the validity of a will was the question in dispute. On the one side the testator was alleged to have been perfectly capable, and on the other side that he was perfectly incapable, of understanding the nature of the act he was doing. Eminent advocates and hard-swearing witnesses abounded on both sides.

One witness swore that the testator, in his opinion, was of sound mind, memory and understanding. He gave his evidence fairly, and seemed desirous of establishing the will. He was then cross-examined in the following manner:

> *Q.* I believe you were related to the testator, were you?
> *A.* I was.

---

[1] *The Forum; or Forty Years Full Practice at the Philadelphia Bar,* vol. I, Philadelphia, 1856, lxxix. My emphasis.
[2] *Ibid.* My emphasis.
[3] *The Art of Winning Cases or Modern Advocacy,* New York and Albany, 1894, 170-172.

Q. Nearly related?

A. Yes.

Q. And would have an interest in the will if established?

A. Yes.

According to Hardwicke,[4] if the advocate had asked nothing further, it was a good point made, and certainly would have materially affected the value of evidence as to the soundness of the testator's mind, because the witness had a direct interest in establishing the will. But in spite of the remonstrance of his junior, as Hardwicke remarks,[5] the leader continued his cross-examination, and asked: "Would you take as much as ten thousand pounds if the will were established?" "I should" said the witness; and, as the newspapers reported "there was profound sensation in court".

Hardwicke further observes: "[o]f course, if matters could have remained here, the profundity of the sensation would have been permanent."[6] However, watchful counsel on the other side quietly remarked: "Just one question."

Q. Have you made a calculation as to what you would be entitled to in the event of an intestacy?

A. I have.

Q. What would it be?

A. As next of kin I should be entitled to fifty thousand pounds.[7]

The above illustration shows that THE CROSS-EXAMINER SHOULD BE AWARE OF THE DANGER OF THE CROSS-EXAMINATION BEING TOO MINUTE AND CIRCUMSTANTIAL. AND HE SHOULD BE AWARE OF

---

[4] *Op. cit.* 171.

[5] *Ibid.*

[6] *Op. cit.* 172.

[7] *Ibid.*

THE FACT THAT THROUGH A SMALL OPENING IN CROSS-EXAMINATION A RE-EXAMINATION ON THE SAME POINT MAY BE ADMITTED.

Remember

- *The cross-examiner must always be watchful.*
- *He must never undervalue his adversary.*
- *He should be aware of the danger of the cross-examination being too minute and circumstantial. And he should be aware of the fact that through a small opening in cross-examination a re-examination on the same point may be admitted.*

DO NOT LOSE YOUR TEMPER

Principle #15

THE CROSS-EXAMINER MUST NEVER LOSE HIS TEMPER

The cross-examiner must never lose his temper. On this principle, which he numbers as his sixth principle of cross-examination, Brown says the following:

> If the witness determine to be witty or refractory with you, you had better settle that account with him at first, or its items will increase with the examination. Let him have an opportunity of satisfying himself, either that he has mistaken your power, or his own. BUT, IN ANY RESULT, BE CAREFUL THAT YOU DO NOT LOSE YOUR TEMPER. ANGER IS ALWAYS, EITHER THE PRECURSOR OR EVIDENCE OF ASSURED DEFEAT IN ANY INTELLECTUAL CONFLICT.[1]

Remember

- *The cross-examiner must never lose his temper.*

---

[1] *The Forum; or Forty Years Full Practice at the Philadelphia Bar,* vol. I, Philadelphia, 1856, lxxix. My emphasis.

DUTIES
DUTIES
DUTIES

Principle #16

THE CROSS-EXAMINER MUST RESPECT THE COURT, BE KIND TO HIS COLLEAGUE, CIVIL TO HIS ANTAGONIST BUT NEVER SACRIFICE THE DUTY TO HIS CLIENT.

HE MUST NEVER BE UNMINDFUL OF HIS DIGNITY.

THE CROSS-EXAMINER MUST NEVER USE IMMORAL OR UNETHICAL PRACTICES.

Brown in his book[1] enunciates as his last principle of cross-examination (the ninth):

> Be respectful to the court and the jury – kind to your colleague – civil to your antagonist – but never sacrifice the slightest principle of duty to an overweening deference towards either.

From this passage it is clear that above all the duties of the advocate the most important is the duty to his client.

Brown also says that the advocate must never be unmindful of his dignity. To use his own words which are employed to describe his third principle of cross-examination:

> Be mild with the mild – shrewd with the crafty – confiding with the honest – merciful to the young, the frail or the fearful – rough to the ruffian, and a thunderbolt to the liar. BUT IN ALL THIS, NEVER BE UNMINDFUL OF YOUR OWN DIGNITY. Bring to bear all the powers of your mind, not that you may shine, but THAT VIRTUE MAY TRIUMPH, AND YOUR CASE MAY PROSPER.[2]

As has been seen before[3] the cross-examiner must follow the principles of morality when conducting a cross-examination.

Hardwicke[4] refers to Judge Elliot,[5] the able and learned writer upon the subject of advocacy, who deals with some immoral or unethical practices of cross-examination which must be avoided. These are the following[6]:

---

[1] *The Forum or Forty Years Full Practice at the Philadelphia Bar,* vol. I, Philadelphia, 1856, lxxx.
[2] *Op. cit.* lxxviii. My emphasis.
[3] See pp. 116, 171 *post.*
[4] *The Art of Winning Cases or Modern Advocacy,* New York and Albany, 1894, 177-179.
[5] No mention however is made to any specific work.
[6] The numbering of them is mine.

(1)"It is a common practice for some not over scrupulous advocates to ask unfair questions. Even so great, and usually so fair an advocate as Erskine was admonished to give the witness fair play. Fair play every witness is entitled to, and fair play the counsel who calls him should see that he gets."[7]

(2) "It is no unusual thing to assume that the witness has made a statement that he did not make, and on this false assumption harass and confuse him. A witness, be it always remembered, is not generally self-possessed under the fire of a hot cross-examination, and may be bewildered by such an assumption made, as most often it is, with a dogmatic and determined air. Such assumptions counsel has no right to make."[8]

(3) "More unfair and more perplexing to the witness, as well as more difficult for the advocate to detect, are those insidious questions in which the assumption is covertly made. It is no uncommon thing for cross-examiners to bewilder witnesses by questions which covertly assume a fact that dare not be openly assumed. ... To this class belong such questions as: When did you cease to be the enemy of the plaintiff? When did you sell your interest in this claim? When did you retire from the conspiracy? When did you convert the horse?"[9]

(4) "This unfair method of examination sometimes takes the form of a question which, in appearance, is one question only, demanding simply a categorical answer, whereas, in reality, several questions are combined. This is an old fallacy, and ought to be so well known as to be readily exposed, but it does, nevertheless, yet do no little mischief. Many a witness has been sorely puzzled by being required to answer 'yes' or 'no' to a question which in form is single, but in fact is double. Thus, a witness is asked: 'You hurt yourself

---

[7] Hardwicke, *op. cit.* 177.
[8] *Ibid.*
[9] *Op. cit.* 177-178.

by jumping off a train running forty miles an hour?' Or he is asked· 'You paid the money to the plaintiff's agent?' Or again he is asked: 'You were the plaintiff's partner in the venture?' If the one to whom are addressed questions so plainly double as these were cool and collected, doubtless he would not be misled; but few witnesses can be cool and collected under cross-examination, and they are often betrayed into error. A witness who has an advocate demanding of him, 'Answer yes or no, sir,' is not in a condition to clearly perceive the unfairness of the question asked him. Nor are the questions ordinarily asked of witnesses so plainly double as these we have given by way of illustration, for many are so adroitly constructed as to deceive keen thinkers. The remedy for this evil is that proposed by Aristotle[10]: 'Several questions,' he says, 'should be at once decomposed into their several parts. Only a single question admits of a single answer.' We commend this advice to our readers. They will find it useful in practice."[11]

Remember

- *The cross-examiner must respect the Court, be kind to his colleague, civil to his antagonist, but never sacrifice the slightest principle of his duty to his client to any of the above duties.*
- *The cross-examiner must never be unmindful of his dignity.*
- *The cross-examiner must never use immoral or unethical practices.*

---

[10] See on this Serghides, *The Technique of Cross-Examination, the Golden Rules of Cross-Examination and Four Masters of Antiquity, two Greek (Socrates and Aristotle) and two Latin (Cicero and Quintilian)*, (in Greek), Nicosia, 2007, vol. 7 of *Studies in Cyprus Law*, 30-31.
[11] *Op. cit.* 178-179.

SMILING OVER SAVAGE STYLE

Principle #17

**THE SMILING STYLE OF CROSS-EXAMINATION
SHOULD BE PREFERRED
TO THE SAVAGE STYLE.**

**START WITH A TONE OF FRIENDLINESS
AND A SMILE.**

Cox[1] and Hardwicke[2] say that there are two styles or modes of cross-examination, the *savage* style and the *smiling* style. Both of them you may see exemplified in any court where you may happen to spend a day.[3]

As Cox elucidates "[t]he aim of the savage style is to *terrify* the witness into telling the truth; the aim of the smiling style is to *win* him to a confession."[4]

Indeed, as the same author testifies the savage style is by far the most frequently in use, especially by young lawyers "who probably imagine that a frown and fierce voice are proof of power".[5] And he goes on to make these remarkable comments, favouring, of course, the smiling style:

> Great is their mistake. The passions rouse the passions. Anger, real or assumed, kindles anger. An attack stimulates to defiance. By showing suspicion of a witness you insult his self-love – you make him your enemy at once – you arm his resolution to resist you – to defy you – to tell you no more than he is obliged to tell – to defeat you, if he can. Undoubtedly there are cases where such a tone is called for; where it is politic as well as just; but they are *rare,* so rare that they should be deemed entirely exceptional. In every part of an Advocate´s career, good temper and self-command are essential qualifications; but in none more so than in the practice of cross-examination. It is marvelous how much may be accomplished with the most difficult witnesses simply by good humour and a smile; a *tone* of friendliness will often succeed in obtaining a reply which has been obstinately denied to a surly aspect and a threatening or reproachful voice. As a general rule, subject to such very rare exceptions as scarcely to enter into your

---

[1] *The Advocate, His Training, Practice, Rights and Duties,* vol. I, London, 1852, 376-377.
[2] *The Art of Winning Cases or Modern Advocacy,* 1894, 152.
[3] Cox, *op. cit.* 376.
[4] *Op. cit.* 376-377.
[5] *Op. cit.* 377.

calculations, you should begin your cross-examination
with an encouraging look, and manner, and phrase.
Remember that the witness knows you to be *on the other
side*; he is prepared to deal with you as an enemy; he
anticipates a badgering; he thinks you are going to trip him
up, if you can; he has to more or less extent, girded
himself for the strife. It is amusing to mark the instant
change in the demeanour of most witnesses, when their
own Counsel has resumed his seat and the Advocate on the
other side rises to cross-examine. The position, the
countenance, plainly show what is passing in the mind.
Either there is fear, or, more often, defiance. If you look
fierce and speak sternly, it is just what had been expected,
and you are met by corresponding acts of self-defence.
But, if instead of this, you wear a pleasant smile, speak in a
kindly tone, use the language of a friendly questioner,
appear to give credit for a desire to tell the whole truth and
nothing but the truth, you surprise, you disarm him: it was
not what he had anticipated; he was prepared to resist an
open enemy, but not to combat a friend; he hesitates what
to do, how to treat you; the fortress is surrendered, he
submits, and answers frankly to your questionings."[6]

Ballantine observes[7] that what is called severe cross-
examination, when applied to a truthful witness, only makes
the truth stand out more clearly. Ballantine in another part of
his book gives an instance where he used the severe method
of cross-examination without managing to uncover an
untruthful witness:

> I cannot forbear relating an anecdote in connection
> with one of the most amiable and excellent of judges, the
> late Lord Hatherley, when he was Vice-Chancellor. I was
> counsel before him, and had to cross-examine a very
> plausible, but certainly not truthful witness. I did so with

[6] *Op. cit.* 377-378.
[7] *Some Experiences of a Barrister's Life,* vol. I., London, 1882, 126.

some severity, and I imagine that I should have been successful before the jury.

His Lordship, however, was of a different opinion, and was much struck with the ingenuousness of the young man, and he evidently thought that he had been exposed to a cruel ordeal. As the witness himself was going out of the court he was heard to whisper to a friend 'Why, the old gent believed every word I swore.'[8]

Remember

- *Smiling style should be preferred to savage style.*
- *Start with a kindly tone and a smile. Avoid harrying the witness save in exceptional cases.*

---

[8] *Op. cit.* 130. As Ballantine says in a footnote the term applied to his Lordship was not of so refined a description.

PURPOSE

PURPOSE

PURPOSE

Principle #18

FIRST YOU WILL RESOLVE WHETHER YOU SHOULD CROSS-EXAMINE AT ALL.

NEVER CROSS-EXAMINE WITHOUT A PURPOSE.

THREE OBJECTS OF CROSS-EXAMINATION.

Ballantine states the following as regards aimless cross-examination:

> An unskillful use of it, on the contrary has a tendency to uphold rather than destroy. If the principles upon which cross-examination ought to be founded are not understood and acted upon, it is worse than useless, <u>and it becomes an instrument against its employer</u>. <u>The reckless asking of a number of questions on the chance of getting at something is too often a plan adopted by unskillful advocates</u>, and NOISE IS MISTAKEN FOR ENERGY. Mr. Baron Alderson once remarked to a counsel of this type, 'Mr. ------, you seem to think that the art of cross-examination is to examine crossly.'[1]

Similarly, Hardwicke[2] remarks that Sir James Scarlett once said of Mr. Topping, an eminent leader on the same circuit, that his idea of cross-examination was putting over again every question asked in chief in a very angry tone, and this appears to be the idea the young members of the bar seem to have of it.

When beginning cross-examining a witness, the following questions may strike the mind of the cross-examiner: Where shall I start? What order shall I follow? Shall I carry him in his examination-in-chief, or begin at the end of it and go backwards, or dodge him about, now here, now there, without method?

Cox asserts[3] that each of these plans has its advantages, and perhaps each should be adopted pursuant to the SPECIAL CIRCUMSTANCES OF THE PARTICULAR CASE.

---

[1] *Some Experiences of a Barrister's Life,* vol. I, London, 1882, 124.

[2] *The Art of Winning Cases or Modern Advocacy,* New York and Albany, 1894, 143.

[3] *The Advocate, His Training, Practice, Rights and Duties,* vol. I, 1852, 378.

Nevertheless, as he says, cross-examining counsel cannot determine which plan to adopt unless he has some DEFINITE DESIGN in the questions he is about to put.[4] Cox underlines that A MERE AIMLESS, HAZARD cross-examination, alas frequently occurring, is a fault which young counsel should most strenuously guard against.[5] According to him, it is much better for cross-examining counsel TO SAY NOTHING than to risk the consequence of random shots, which may, as usually happens, wound his friends and his opponents.[6] Subsequently, Cox describes the bad and erroneous practice of lawyers in court in conducting aimless and hazard cross-examination:

> Very little experience in Civil and Criminal Courts, and in the latter especially, will assure you that there is no error so common as this. Some persons seem to suppose that their credit is concerned in getting up a cross-examination, and they look upon the dismissal of a witness without it, as if it were an opportunity lost, and they fear that clients will attribute it, not so much to prudence as to conscious incapacity. So they rise and put a number of questions that do not concern the issue, and perhaps elicit something more damaging to their own cause than anything the other side has brought out, and the result is, that they leave their case in a far worse condition than before.[7]

Next to this passage and as a result of it, Cox states one important principle of cross-examination: *"NEVER TO CROSS-EXAMINE UNLESS YOU HAVE SOME DISTINCT OBJECT TO GAIN BY IT."*[8]

---

[4] *Ibid.*
[5] *Op. cit.* 378-379.
[6] *Op. cit.* 379.
[7] *Ibid.*
[8] *Ibid.* Italics belong to Cox, capitals belong to me.

And he further explains that it is far better for the cross-examiner to be mute through the whole trial, dismissing every witness without a word than, for the MERE SAKE OF APPEARANCES, to ply him with questions that ARE NOT THE RESULT OF A PURPOSE.[9] The cross-examiner will not fall in the estimation of those on whom his fortunes will depend; but the contrary. He goes on to say that attorneys well know that "in legal conflicts, even more than in military ones, DISCRETION is the better part of valour; they will not mistake the motive of your silence, but they commend the prudence whose wisdom is proved by the results."[10]

After this passage, the said author comes to the conclusion that the first resolve of the cross-examiner will be WHETHER HE SHOULD CROSS-EXAMINE AT ALL.[11]

Cox admits that it is impossible to prescribe any rules to guide cross-examining attorney in this.[12] So much, as he says, DEPENDS ON THE PARTICULAR CIRCUMSTANCES OF EACH CASE.[13] His advice is that the cross-examiner must rely upon his SAGACITY, "on a hasty review of what the witness has said", how his testimony has affected his case, and what probability there is of him weakening it.[14] If the witness said nothing material, it is often the safer course for the cross-examiner to let him go down unless he is instructed that the witness can give some testimony in the attorney's favour or damaging to the party who has called him.[15] However, unless the advocate is so instructed, he should not on some mere vague suspicions of his own, or in hope of hitting a blot somewhere by accident, incur the hazard of detaining the witness or eliciting something that may damage

---

[9] *Ibid.*
[10] *Ibid.* My emphasis.
[11] *Ibid.*
[12] *Op. cit.* 380.
[13] *Ibid.*
[14] *Ibid.*
[15] *Ibid.*

him – a result which is, as Cox observes, to be seen every day in our courts.[16]

Cox correctly alleges that, as a general rule, it is dangerous to cross-examine a witness called for mere formalities, as to prove signatures, attestations, copies, and such like.[17] However, such witnesses are not to be immediately dismissed, for the cross-examiner should first consider if there be any parts of his case which they may prove, so as to save a witness for him. Then he should confine himself to the purpose for which he has detained them.[18]

Ballantine[19] states that in equity cases, the notion of cross-examination is ludicrous; it has, however, the merit of being thoroughly inoffensive. He goes on thus:

> I have heard two or three specimens of it. In these cases the witnesses had filed affidavits which the adverse counsel examined from, and made them repeat orally what they had already sworn to, as if the object of the process was to obtain from the mouth of the witness in court what had already been put upon paper in the solicitor's office.[20]

According to Cox, in deciding whether to cross-examine a witness, it is necessary for the cross-examiner to remember that there can be but THREE OBJECTS in cross-examination:

> (a) To DESTROY or WEAKEN the force of the evidence the witness has already given against his client.
> (b) To ELICIT something in favour of his client, which the witness has not stated.

---

[16] *Ibid.*
[17] *Ibid.*
[18] *Ibid.*
[19] *Some Experiences of a Barrister's Life,* vol. I., London, 1882, 127.
[20] *Ibid.*

(c) To DISCREDIT the witness, by showing to the
Jury, from his past history or present demeanour, that he is
unworthy of belief.[21]

As Cox emphasizes "NEVER SHOULD YOU ENTER
UPON A CROSS-EXAMINATION WITHOUT HAVING A
CLEAR PURPOSE TO PURSUE ONE OR ALL OF THESE
OBJECTS. IF YOU HAVE NOT SUCH, KEEP YOUR
SEAT."[22]

These three objects of cross-examination are mentioned
also by Hardwicke.[23]

In the following chapters we shall deal with these three
objects in cross-examination as explained by Cox, dealing at
the same time with the tactics used by cross-examiners in
relation to each of these objects.

Cox in ending his chapter on cross-examination returns again
to its purpose, which he considers very important, and says:

> In concluding these remarks on *cross-examination,* the
> rarest, the most useful, and the most difficult to be
> acquired of the accomplishments of the Advocate, we
> would again urge upon your attention the importance of
> CALM DISCRETION. In addressing a Jury, you may
> sometimes talk without having anything to say, and no
> harm will come of if. But in cross-examination, every
> question that does not advance your case injures it. IF
> YOU HAVE NOT DEFINITE OBJECT TO ATTAIN,
> DISMISS THE WITNESS WITHOUT A WORD.[24]

---

[21] *Op. cit.* 380-381.
[22] *Op. cit.* 381. My emphasis.
[23] *The Art of Winning Cases or Modern Advocacy,* New York and Albany,
1894, 152.
[24] *Op. cit.* 433. My capitals but not my italics.

Remember

- First the cross-examiner will decide whether he should cross-examine at all.
- He should never enter upon a cross-examination without having a clear purpose to pursue.
- If he cannot pursue one or all of the three objects mentioned above,[25] it is better to keep his seat.
- Above all the advocate must show calm discretion.

---

[25] At p. 95 *ante*.

PURPOSE
PURPOSE
PURPOSE

Principle #18.1

First Object and Tactics

TO *DESTROY* OR *WEAKEN* THE FORCE OF THE WITNESS'S TESTIMONY IN FAVOUR OF THE OTHER SIDE

Cox says that if the design of the cross-examiner is to destroy
or weaken the force of the witness's testimony in favour of his
side, he can attain it only by one of two processes.[1] He must
show from the witness's own lips that what he has stated is:

(a) FALSE, or
(b) capable of EXPLANATION.[2]

WHERE THE AIM IS TO SHOW THAT WHAT HE HAS STATED IS FALSE

Cox says:

> If your opinion be that he is honest, but prejudiced; that he
> is mistaken; that he has formed a too hasty judgment and
> so forth, your bearing towards him cannot be [but] too
> gentle, kind, and conciliatory. Approach him with a smile,
> encourage him with a cheering word, assure him that you
> are satisfied that he intends to tell the truth, and the whole
> truth, and having thus won his good will and confidence,
> proceed slowly, quietly, and in a tone as *conversational* as
> possible, to his object.[3]

Furthermore, Cox's advice is for the advocate not to
approach the witness too suddenly because otherwise he will
frighten him "with that which forms the greatest impediment
to the discovery of the truth from witnesses, *the dread of
appearing to contradict themselves.*"[4] And he goes on to say
that if once the alarm be kindled, it is extremely difficult to

---

[1] *The Advocate, His Training, Practice, Rights, and Duties,* vol. I,
London, 1852, 381.
[2] *Ibid.*
[3] *Ibid.*
[4] *Ibid.*

procure from the witness plain and unequivocal answers. This is so according to him because the witness forthwith places himself ON THE DEFENSIVE, and, considering cross-examining lawyer as his enemy, tries to weaken whatever may drop from him.[5]

What is now the better course to follow with such a witness? Cox's advice is to start "with the beginning of the witness's story and conduct him through it again in the same order, only introducing at the right places the questions which are intended to explain or qualify what he has stated in his examination in chief."[6] As he observes, the advantage of this course consists in its avoidance on any appearance of a surprise upon him. He also remarks that the cross-examiner must take the witness into his former track.[7] He must even make him repeat a portion of what he has said before and recall his mind to the subject with which it is familiar.[8] So the scene is again before him, occupying his thoughts.[9] *"Then"* as Cox states, "it is easy to try him upon the details (but still gently), to suggest whether it may not have differed by so and so from that which he has described, or if so and so (which gives to the transaction another complexion) did not occur also, and thus, at more or less length, according to the circumstances of the case."[10]

Then comes a useful warning from Cox. This warning is against exhibiting any kind of EMOTION during cross-examination. More specifically, the cross-examiner must avoid the "slightest show of exultation" when the witness answers to the advocate's "sagacious touch, and reveals what he had intended to conceal."[11] If this does not occur, the

[5] *Op. cit.* 381-382.
[6] *Op. cit.* 382.
[7] *Ibid.*
[8] *Ibid.*
[9] *Ibid.*
[10] *Ibid.*
[11] *Ibid.*

advocate will often face this embarrassing situation: It "starts him into self-command and closes the portal of his mind" against the cross-examining advocate more resolutely than ever. The advocate has put him upon his guard and defeated himself (i.e. the advocate). And then comes the most valuable advice:

> LET THE MOST IMPORTANT ANSWER *APPEAR* TO
> BE RECEIVED AS CALMLY AND UNCONSCIOUSLY
> AS IF IT WERE THE MOST TRIVIAL OF GOSSIP.[12]

Lastly, on this point Cox states that in the same manner the cross-examiner may carry the witness to the conclusion of his story "and what with an explanation of one fact, and addition to another, and *toning down* of the colour of the whole, the evidence will usually appear in a very different aspect, after a judicious cross-examination, from that which it wore at the close of the examination-in-chief."[13]

In connection with one of the cases we are dealing here, specifically when the cross-examiner suspects that some statements are FALSE in FACT, although not wilfully misstated, such as errors of the senses, or of the imagination or of the memory, the task of the cross-examiner becomes "a very difficult one".[14] This is so because it is not wise for the cross-examiner to charge the witness with perjury nor to let him understand that he does not believe him. Witnesses are very sensitive to self-contradiction and usually they suspect the purpose of the cross-examiner instantly and dread being made to appear as lying. More often they arm their resolution to adhere to their original statement without qualification or explanation.[15]

---

[12] *Op. cit.* 382-383. My capitals but not my italics.
[13] *Op. cit.* 383.
[14] *Ibid.*
[15] *Op. cit.* 383-384.

The advice of Cox to the lawyers in such cases is to show from the witness's own lips that he was MISTAKEN by using the extremest caution in approaching him.[16] According to Cox, the tactics to be employed by cross-examining counsel are these:

> You must wear an open brow and assume a kindly tone. Let there be no *sound of suspicion* in your language. Intimate to him delicately your confidence that he is sincerely desirous of telling the truth and the whole truth. Be careful not to frighten him by point-blank questions that go at once to involve him in a contradiction, or he will see your design and thwart it by a resolute adhesion to his first assertion. YOU MUST APPROACH THE OBJECT UNDER COVER, OPENING WITH SOME QUESTIONS THAT RELATE TO ANOTHER MATTER, AND THEN GRADUALLY COMING ROUND TO THE DESIRED POINT. And even when you have neared it you must endeavour, by every devise your ingenuity can suggest to avoid the direct question, the answer to which necessarily and obviously involves the contradiction THE SAFER AND SURER COURSE IS TO BRING OUT THE DISCREPANCY BY INFERENCE, THAT IS, INSTEAD OF SEEKING TO MAKE THE WITNESS *UNSAY* WHAT HE HAS SAID, IT SHOULD BE YOUR AIM TO ELICIT A STATEMENT WHICH MAY BE SHOWN BY ARGUMENT TO BE INCONSISTENT WITH THE FORMER STATEMENT.[17]

Cox clarifies that it must be understood that in all this the cross-examiner's duty is to ascertain the very truth by tracing an error without trying to entrap an honest though erred witness into a falsehood or throw him to perplexity with the

---

[16] *Op. cit.* 384.
[17] *Ibid.* My capitals but not my italics.

<u>aim to discredit him</u>[18]. And then Cox comes to the RULES OF MORALITY:

> Your duty as an Advocate is strictly limited by the rules of morality. It is no more permissible for you to tamper with the truth of others…. than to be false yourself.[19]

WHERE THE AIM IS TO SHOW THAT WHAT HE HAS STATED IS CAPABLE OF EXPLANATION

Surely, as Cox points out, an explanation of the statements of a witness is easier to be procured from him than is a contradiction. This is so, as in the former case "there is not the same formidable fear of being presented to the Court in the *aspect* of one who is perjured".[20]

He further maintains:

> A witness who is conscious that he has been induced, by the encouraging examination of his own counsel, to say too much, IS OFTEN READY to seize the opportunity afforded by cross-examination TO MODIFY his assertions by qualifications and explanations. IF YOU SEE THIS TENDENCY, *which is usually shown at the beginning*, you have only to encourage it by falling in with his mood, and carefully avoiding anything calculated to make him fear the use to which you may put his admissions.[21]

---

[18] *Op. cit.* 384-385.
[19] *Op. cit.* 385.
[20] *Ibid.*
[21] *Ibid.* My capitals and my italics.

On the other hand, If the cross-examiner does not see such tendency, Cox recommends the following:

> IF THERE BE NO SUCH TENDENCY, then your course will be the reverse of that to be pursued when you are seeking contradictions. Instead of avoiding the point, you should go at once to that part of the evidence, repeat the very question, and when you have received the same reply, follow it with a series of questions *as to the circumstances* which, as you are instructed, *go to modify or explain* the statements you are combating.[22]

Cox further supports that if the cross-examiner is satisfied that the witness is honest and truthful he must let his questions be as LEADING as he can frame them, naming the fact, and in such a form that the answer shall be a plain "YES" or "NO".[23] And then comes a warning that the cross-examiner should be cautious not to press his inquiries too far.[24] Cox ends this section of his treatise by making the following points which need to be kept in mind by any cross-examiner:

> Having obtained enough for your purpose, PASS ON. You may obtain *too much*. THERE IS NO MORE USEFUL FACULTY IN THE PRACTICE OF AN ADVOCATE THAN TO KNOW *WHEN HE HAS DONE ENOUGH*. Many cases are lost BY SAYING TOO MUCH THAN BY NOT SAYING SUFFICIENT.[25]

This advice "WHEN TO SIT DOWN" is to me the most important of all.

---

[22] *Op. cit.* 385-386. My capitals and my italics.
[23] *Op. cit.* 386.
[24] *Ibid.*
[25] *Ibid.*

Hardwicke suitably observes that while witnesses are sworn to tell "the truth, the WHOLE truth, and nothing but the truth," yet there are witnesses who believe that they <u>are not obliged to tell anything they are not asked about</u>, and if they are undesirous of telling all they know, they will give evasive answers UNTIL ASKED ABOUT THE PARTICULAR THING THEY WISH TO CONCEAL, and then they will withhold it no longer. Hardwicke then refers to an amusing instance which illustrates what he means, which is given by one of the leading Reviews:[26]

Some time ago the writer, while waiting in court, watched the trial of a case where the plaintiff sought to recover damages for a breach of warranty. The defendant had sold him a horse with an express warranty that he was sound and kind and free from all 'outs'. The next day the plaintiff noticed that the shoe was loose, and he undertook to drive him into a blacksmith's shop to have him shod, when the horse exhibited such violent reluctance that he was obliged to abandon the attempt. Repeated efforts made it evident that he never would be shod willingly, and therefore he was obliged to sell him. The defendant called two witnesses. The first, an honest, clean looking man, testified that he was a blacksmith, that he knew the horse in question perfectly well, and he had shod him about the time referred to in plaintiff's testimony. 'Did you have any difficulty in shoeing him?' ask the defendant's counsel. 'Not the least. He stood perfectly quiet. Never had a horse stand quieter.' The other, a venerable-looking man, with a clear blue eye, testified that he had owned the horse that he was perfectly quiet. 'Did you ever have any trouble about getting him into a blacksmith's shop?' 'Well, sir, I don't remember that I ever had occasion to carry him to a blacksmith's shop while I owned him.' The plaintiff's counsel evidently thought that cross-examination would only develop this unpleasant testimony more strongly, so

---

[26] 10 *American Law Review,* 153, footnote.

he let the witnesses go. The jury found for the defendant. The next morning, as the writer was sitting in court waiting for a verdict, a man behind him, whom he recognized as the blacksmith, leaned forward and said: 'You heard that horse case tried yesterday, didn't you? Well, that fellow who tried the case for the plaintiff didn't know how to cross-examine worth a cent. I told him that the horse stood perfectly quiet while I shod him; and so he did. I did not tell him I had to hold him by the nose with a pair of pincers to make him stand. The old man said he never took him to a blacksmith's shop while he had him. No more he did. He had to take him out into an open lot and cast him before he could shoe him.'[27]

Remember

•   *Where the aim is to show that what the witness has stated is false the cross-examiner must approach him amicably and slowly. When the statement is false in fact the cross-examiner must bring out the discrepancy by inference.*

•   *The cross-examiner must never seek to entrap an honest witness.*

•   *Where the aim is to show that what the witness has stated is capable of explanation the course to be followed by the cross-examiner depends on whether he sees the witness has the tendency to modify his assertions. If he does have such a tendency, the advocate must encourage him to make the necessary modifications. If not, the advocate must ask him again the very question and when he receives the same reply must ask him about the circumstances of the case which may go to modify or explain the statements. In this procedure the advocate must proceed by using leading questions. Having obtained enough for his purpose, the advocate must sit down.*

---

[27] Hardwicke, *op. cit.* 149-151.

PURPOSE

PURPOSE

PURPOSE

Principle #18.2

Second Object and Tactics

TO *ELICIT* SOMETHING IN YOUR FAVOUR

As we have seen, the second object of cross-examination is to procure something in favour of the cross-examining counsel's side, which the witness has not stated.[1]

Cox says that the method to elicit something in your favour will depend upon the character of the witness,[2] and the distinction to follow must be observed.

If the cross-examiner believes that the witness is honest and truthful he may "PROCEED DIRECTLY to the subject matter with PLAIN, POINT-BLANK QUESTIONS".[3]

If the cross-examiner suspects that the witness will not readily state what he is aware will operate on the advocate's side, the advocate must approach him "with some of the precautions requisite for the cross-examination of a witness who is not trustworthy."[4] Since the cross-examiner intends to elicit from the witness something in favour of his client's side, it is not wise to discredit him, by showing him to be unworthy of belief, without losing the advantage of his testimony on his own behalf. So, as Cox states the cross-examiner cannot venture to prove the witness by contradiction.[5] He then explains how the cross examiner may attain his end:

> You can only do by GRADUAL APPROACHES. ...[T]he surest course is to conduct him to the end by almost imperceptible degrees. Elicit one small fact, perhaps but remotely connected with the main object of your inquiry. HE MAY NOT SEE THE CHAIN OF CONNECTION, and will answer *that question* freely; or deem it not worth evading. A very small admission usually requires another to confirm or explain. Having said so much, the witness cannot stop there; he *must* go on, in self-defence, and thus,

---

[1] Cox, *The Advocate, His Training, Practice, Rights, and Duties,* vol. I., 1852, 386.
[2] *Ibid.*
[3] *Ibid.* My emphasis.
[4] *Op. cit.* 386.
[5] *Op. cit.* 386-387.

by judicious approaches, you bring him to the main point. Even if then he should turn upon you, and say no more, you will have done enough to satisfy the Jury that HIS SILENCE IS AS SIGNIFICANT as would have been his confession.[6]

PROFITING BY WITNESS'S SILENCE

The next important thing with which Cox deals is the importance of the SILENCE of the witness. He well observes that "A REFUSAL TO ANSWER, OR AN EVASION OF YOUR QUESTION, WILL FREQUENTLY BE MORE SERVICEABLE TO YOU THAN HIS WORDS."[7] He then says that when the cross-examiner has done enough to satisfy the court that the witness can say something more, if he pleases, he will withdraw and then may suggest by inferences from the witness's silence as may be most advantageous to his case.[8] Cox goes on to say that it is one of the most frequent and fatal faults of young lawyers

THAT THEY *WILL HAVE* AN ANSWER *IN WORDS* TO *EVERY* QUESTION THEY PUT, FORGETTING THAT THE ANSWER MAY BE INJURIOUS, WHILE THE SILENCE MAY BE MORE THAN SUGGESTIVE OF ALL THAT IT IS THEIR DESIGN TO ELICIT.[9]

---

[6] *Op. cit.* 387. My capitals but not by italics.
[7] *Ibid.* My emphasis.
[8] *Op. cit.* 388.
[9] *Op. cit.* 388. My capitals but not my italics.

UNFAVOURABLE ANSWER TO WITNESS

The last point made by Cox in this section is also a very important one. He suggests though he does not say it clearly that the advocate must play the role of an actor when he is faced with an answer by the witness which is not favourable to his client. In his own words:

> The most cautious cross-examination will not always prevent that most disagreeable of incidents to an Advocate, the receipt of an answer that tells strongly against him, when his is anticipating an answer in his favour. When such a *contretemps* occurs, it is most important that *you* SHOULD NOT APPEAR TO BE TAKEN BY SURPRISE. Let neither countenance, nor tone of voice, nor expression of annoyance, show to the spectator that you are conscious of being taken aback. If they laugh, be not vexed; if others exhibit surprise, be as calm and appear as satisfied as if *you* HAVE EXPECTED IT. Thus you will repel the force of the blow, for seeing that you are not perplexed by it, the audience begin to suppose it not to be so important as they deem it to be, or they give you credit for some profounder purpose than apparent, or that you are prepared with a contradiction, or explanation. Sometimes, indeed, where the blow has been more than usually staggering, it may not be bad policy to weaken its force by openly making light of it, repeating it, taking a note of it, or appending a joke to it. At to no time is self-command more requisite to an Advocate than such a moment, and never is the contrast between experience and inexperience, the prudent and the injudicious, more palpably exhibited.[10]

---

[10] *Op. cit.* 388-389. My capitals but not my italics.

Remember

- *The method used by the cross-examiner to elicit something depends upon the character of the witness.*
- *If the cross-examiner believes that the witness is honest and truthful he may proceed directly to the subject matter with plain, point-blank questions. If on the other hand he suspects that the witness will not readily state what he is aware will operate to the advocate's advantage, the cross-examiner must approach him gradually, step by step.*
- *A refusal to answer or an evasion of the question will frequently be more serviceable to the cross-examiner's client than the witness's words.*
- *When the cross-examiner is faced with an answer by the witness which is not favourable to his client he should not appear to be taken by surprise. He should be as calm and appear as satisfied as if he has expected it.*

PURPOSE
PURPOSE
PURPOSE

Principle #18.3

Third Object and Tactics

TO *DISCREDIT* THE WITNESS

The third purpose of cross-examination is to discredit the witness. Cox notes that upon so important a matter, we shall at start try to trace some rules which may help to determine the limits of an advocate's duty in his attempt to discredit a witness by cross-examination.[1]

Cross alleges[2] that the broad landmarks of morality should also apply to the legal profession. Such are the dictates of morality, which forbid us to do an injury to our neighbours or to lie for any purpose whatever. Cox rightly believes that the character and credit of the profession would be infinitely raised in public esteem if these broad landmarks of morality were more strictly observed in the practice of advocacy, and he alleges that he is sure that in the long run it would be profitable to the advocate's clients.[3]

He also notes that "bullying and browbeating are as rare now as they were common formerly". He continues: "It is seldom, indeed, that unscrupulous assertions and daring misrepresentations of evidence are indulged. The standard of morality has been advanced among us, and is advancing...."[4]

Cox aptly alleges <u>that the principle that should govern the advocate's conduct</u> in dealing with an adverse witness, with the view to discredit him, <u>should be that which he would recognize in his</u> "<u>private capacity as a *Christian gentleman*</u>, and which may be summed up in three words – JUSTICE, TRUTH, CHARITY".[5] He goes on thus:

> You have *no right* to tempt, or terrify, or entrap him into falsehood. You have *no right* to charge him with falsehood, unless you are in your own mind entirely

---

[1] *The Advocate, His Training, Practice, Rights, and Duties,* vol. I., London, 1852, 389.

[2] Disagreeing, as he says with Lord Brougham and others.

[3] *Op. cit.* 390.

[4] *Op. cit.* 391.

[5] *Op. cit.* 392. My underline but not my italics.

convinced that he is *lying,* and not that he is merely
mistaken.

JUSTICE demands that you deal with him as you
would be dealt with by him, were you the witness and he
the Advocate. TRUTH demands that you make no
endeavour to misrepresent him, or to distort the meaning of
his words, contrary to your own conscientious conviction
of his honesty. CLARITY demands that you put upon his
evidence the construction most accordant with good
intentions.

Only when you are in your mind thoroughly persuaded
that the witness is *not* telling the truth, may you with
propriety use your art to entrap him into contradictions, or
charge him with falsehood in word or manner.[6]

Similarly Hardwicke emphasizes that no self-respecting
advocate will ever try to entrap an honest witness and get him
into trouble which may lead to loss of reputation, even if, by
doing so, he could win the most important cause.[7] Elsewhere
in the same treatise he notes that the cross-examiner should be
careful not to treat an honest witness as if he were dishonest.[8]

PERJURY LESS FREQUENT THAN MISTAKE

Lastly, on this topic Cox asserts that "there is much *less*
of *perjury,* and vastly *more* of *mistake,* in witnesses, than the
unaccustomed observer would imagine to be possible, unless
he studied the physiology of the mind, and had thence learned
how manifold are the sources of error, and how imperfect is

---

[6] *Op. cit.* 392-393.
[7] *The Art of Winning Cases or Modern Advocacy,* New York and Albany,
1894, 160.
[8] *Op. cit.* 179.

the sense that conveys the knowledge of facts, and the understanding that tries, and proves, and applies them."[9]

According to him, to the advocate it is of vital importance that he should attain to the full comprehension of this truth. And that this truth must be "the guiding-star" of his conduct in cross-examining a witness. Moreover, in his view, the consciousness of this truth will govern the advocate's words, his voice, his manner; "change the tone mistrust into that of confidence; the language of rebuke into that of kindness; the eye that flashes anger and kindles defiance into the look that wins to frankness."[10]

Hardwicke rightly says that the following observations of Archbishop Whately, on the unfair treatment of witnesses by counsel, are worthy of consideration:

> I think that the kind of skill by which the cross-examiner succeeds in alarming, misleading or bewildering an honest witness may be characterized as the most, or one of the most, base and depraved of all possible employments of intellectual power. Nor is it by any means the most effectual way of eliciting truth. The mode best adapted for attaining this object is, I am convinced, quite different from that by which an honest, simple-minded witness is most easily baffled and confused. I have seen the experiment tried of subjecting a witness to such a kind of cross-examination by a practical lawyer as would have been, I am convinced, the most likely to alarm and perplex many an honest witness, without any effect in shaking the testimony; and afterward by a totally opposite mode of examination, such as would not at all have perplexed one who was honestly telling the truth, that same witness was drawn on, step by step, to acknowledge the utter falsity of the whole. Generally speaking, a quiet gentle, and straightforward, though full and careful examination will be the most adapted to elicit truth, and maneuvers and the

---

[9] *Op. cit.* 393.
[10] *Op. cit.* 393-394.

brow-beating which are the best adapted to confuse an honest, simple-minded witness are just what the dishonest one is the best prepared for. The more the storm blusters, the more carefully he wraps round him the cloak which a warm sunshine will induce him to throw off.'[11]

Hardwicke says that while he does not agree with all that Whately says especially with what he says upon the treatment of a dishonest witness, his views are valuable as coming from a disinterested observer – a man of ability who was not a lawyer.[12]

In another part of his treatise, Hardwicke remarks that many cases are lost by injudicious attacks upon the credit of witnesses upon cross-examination. He says that parties to causes are often actuated by feelings of the bitterest enmity to each other and allow their passions to cloud their judgments. They become not only intent upon winning their cases, but of destroying the characters of their opponents[13]. As he puts it "[n]o advocate should allow himself to became an instrument of vengeance in the hands of his irate clients".[14] He continues thus:

If he will allow them to do so, they will often dictate to him the questions to be asked upon cross-examination, and will become seriously offended if he does not ask them, but the advocate is unworthy of his profession if he becomes basely subservient to his client under such circumstances. He should plainly tell his client that he cannot submit to such dictation; and that he shall pursue the course which seems to him to be proper.[15]

---

[11] *The Art of Winning Cases or Modern Advocacy,* New York and Albany, 1894, 148.
[12] *Op. cit.* 148-149.
[13] *Op. cit.* 172.
[14] *Ibid.*
[15] *Ibid.*

The same author says that there are times when the credit of a witness should be impeached by showing that from his history he is not a man likely to swear the truth if it becomes to his interest to swear to the contrary; but unless the offence which he has committed, or is supposed to have committed, be of recent occurrence, and of a heinous nature, it would be wiser to ask no questions concerning it.[16] He says also that it is often cruel and inhuman for counsel to unearth errors of conduct which have been committed many years before, and which, perhaps, have been sincerely repented of, by the offender. According to him, it seems to be inexcusable for an advocate to pursue this course and ridicule a human being who is trying to live honestly in the community.[17]

In his view, and rightly so, the advocate must remember that throwing mud is a game that two can play at, and that for a man who lives in a glass house to throw stones is a foolish thing to do. It is usual where one side assails the credit of a witness or party to a cause, the other side, through feelings of revenge, is apt to do the same thing.[18]

Hardwicke also suitably supports the view that with female, youthful, modest or aged witnesses the advocate should deal kindly.[19] He goes on that "[a]s a matter of policy, aside from the inhumanity and cruelty of an opposite course, it is better to pursue this plan, and even if it were not the best policy, an advocate can never afford to do anything unbecoming a gentleman, in the discharge of his duties, whatever they may be."[20]

---

[16] *Op. cit.* 173.
[17] *Ibid.*
[18] *Op. cit.* 174.
[19] *Op. cit.* 152. See also pp. 183-184.
[20] *Op. cit.* 152-153.

WHAT IS MEANT BY DISCREDITING WITNESS

Turning to Cox we shall deal now with the meaning of the phrase "to discredit a witness". He uses it with two meanings as follows:

(a) To show that the witness's evidence is not to be implicitly believed; that he is mistaken in the whole of or in parts of it, that he has been himself deceived, and
(b) To show that the witness is lying or to be perjured.

WHEN THE WITNESS IS MISTAKEN

Cox starts with the first meaning of the phrase, i.e. to show that the evidence of the witness is not to be implicitly believed. By so doing, Cox says, the advocate not only acts in strict accordance with justice, truth, and charity, but is far more likely to attain his object than by charging wilful falsehood or perjury, by which course, if he fails to impress the jury, he endangers his cause.[21]

In regard to the above, Cox states that the following practice in the courts is not rare:

> It not unfrequently happens that a charge of perjury against the witnesses on the other side induces the Jury to make the trial in question of the honour of the witnesses instead of the issue on the record. They say 'if we find for the defendant, after what has been said by his counsel against the plaintiff's witnesses, we shall be confirming his assertion that they are perjured which we do not believe;' and so, to save the characters of their neighbours, they give a verdict against the assailant.[22]

---

[21] *Op. cit.* 394.
[22] *Ibid.*

On the same lines, Hardwicke remarks that the jurors are apt to sympathize with a witness who is unjustly attacked by counsel upon cross-examination, and in making up their verdict are often unconsciously influenced by such improper conduct upon the part of advocates.[23] He also says that juries are quick to resent unwarranted attacks upon the character of witnesses or parties upon cross-examination. Furthermore, in estimating the damages to the plaintiff they will usually give damages for the original wrong which he has suffered at the hands of the defendant, but they will also give him damages which have been done to his character by a virulent cross-examination, or by a malignant attack upon him made by the advocate in his address to the jury.[24]

Cox concludes that "*HONESTY IS WISDOM AS WELL AS VIRTUE*" and this should be treasured in the advocate's memory as a warning against a style of cross-examination once popular but now daily falling more and more into disrepute.[25]

On the same lines, Brown observes the following interesting point:

> Singleness of purpose, clearly expressed, is the best trait in the examination of witnesses – whether they be honest or the reverse. Falsehood is not detected by cunning, but by the light of truth, or if by cunning, it is the cunning of the witness and not of the counsel.[26]

Coming back to Cox, he says that in truth the advocate will find an ample field opened to him to show the weakness and worthlessness of the evidence of a witness. This is done

---

[23] *The Art of Winning Cases or Modern Advocacy,* New York and Albany, 1894, 146.
[24] *Op. cit.* 173.
[25] *Op. cit.* 394-395.
[26] *The Forum; or Forty Years Full Practice at the Philadephia Bar,* Philadephia, vol. I, 1856, lxxix.

by bringing into play all that knowledge of the physiology of the mind and of the value of the evidence which it is presumed that he has acquired in his training, before becoming an advocate.[27]

As he indicates, it often occurs that an unpracticed advocate "arms the witness against him, before he has opened his lips by a certain defiant look and air as he rises from his seat, as if he were already reveling in anticipated triumph over his victim."[28] Besides, he says that "[n]othing is more fatal than this to success in cross-examination, for it provokes the pride of witness, sets him on his guard, and rouses him to resistance. He says in his heart 'You shall get nothing out of me.' And it is probable that nothing you will get."[29]

What should distinguish the advocate when he rises for the cross-examination of a witness? According to Cox: "[a] sober quietness, an expression of good temper, a certain *friendliness* of look and manner" and not "brow-beating", and "frightening into contradictions".[30] The advocate must show that the witness is mistaken and he must begin with conciliation by removing the witness's fear of him. He must let it be understood, as soon as possible, that he is not going to insult him, or to entrap him into falsehood, or to take unfair advantage of him. Further he must let it be believed that he has confidence in his desire to tell the truth and all the truth, and that his aim is to ASCERTAIN THE PRECISE LIMITS OF POSITIVE TRUTH in the story he has told.[31]

Cox then says that the advocate must proceed very gently, until he sees that the witness is reassured, and that good understanding has been established between themselves. Cox

---

[27] *Op. cit.* 395.
[28] *Ibid.*
[29] *Op. cit.* 395-396.
[30] *Op. cit.* 396.
[31] *Ibid.*

says that the advocate must employ smiling questions which elicit smiling answers.[32]

Similarly, Hardwicke[33] in his treatise underlines that at the outset he wishes to impress upon his readers the advantage to be gained by treating hostile witnesses kindly, except in rare cases. He observes thus:

> A writer of experience says upon this point: 'Docility and friendliness of a witness are of the utmost consequence. And courtesy toward him is a probable means to obtain and keep him; courtesy in words, voice and manner. Rudeness and incivility toward him is very likely to put him out of temper, and to make him lay back his ears.
>
> Little peculiarities of his nature must be humored; his sense of personal dignity must not be offended; if he be deaf, or have an impediment in his speech, this infirmity must not be a subject of merriment; and if his voice be naturally or from timidity low, he should be gently, not roughly, exhorted to speak up. So, if the witness exhibit [sic] any clownish or awkward habit or manner, it may be better to let it pass unnoticed than to attempt to correct it.'[34]

Hardwicke in another part of his treatise explains the technique of conducting a cross-examination used by Sir James Scarlett, an accomplished advocate, which fully corresponds to the method described in the above passage. Hardwicke highly recommends to his readers this method of Scarlett:

> 'In cross-examination, he outstrips all that have ever appeared at the British bar; not, perhaps, in any one single quality – for while some have excelled him in strength and

---

[32] *Ibid.*

[33] *The Art of Winning Cases or Modern Advocacy,* New York and Albany, 1894, 146.

[34] *Op. cit.* 146.

force, others have left him behind them in craft and wit. His superiority, however, as an accomplished cross-examiner – as one combining the best qualities for the office, and making the best use of them at the best time and to best effect – must on every hand be admitted. His brow is never clothed with terror, and his hand never aims to grasp the thunderbolt; but the gentlemanly ease, the polished courtesy and the Christian urbanity and affection, with which he proceeds to the task, do infinitely more mischief to the testimony of witnesses who are striving to deceive, or upon whom he finds it expedient to fasten a suspicion. He has often thrown the most careful and cunning off their guard, by the very behavior from which they inferred their security. Seldom has he discouraged a witness by harshness, and never by insult; and to put men upon the defensive by a hostile attitude he has always considered unwise and unsafe. Hence he takes those he has to examine, as it were by the hand; makes them friends, enters into familiar conversation with them, encourages them to tell him what will best answer his purpose, and thus secures a victory without appearing to commence a conflict.'[35]

Hardwicke refers also to the remarks made by the learned Sir William David Evans upon the subject of cross-examination. The most worthy of note as to these remarks is the observation made by Sir William David Evans - *the cross-examiner, while he is a protector of a private right, is also the minister of public justice*. So the adoption by him of an unfair conduct in cross-examination has often an effect repugnant to the interests which it professes to promote.[36]

Hardwicke aptly supports the view that courts and juries appreciate delicacy of feeling upon the part of advocates. He further says that where in cross-examination it becomes important to inquire into the past history of a witness, or to

---

[35] *Op. cit.* 233-234.
[36] *Op. cit.* 236.

speak about the death of a near relative or dear friend, or to touch some chord of sorrow, it is wise to use introductory expressions deploring the necessity of asking such questions, and representing it as one of the unpleasant but imperative duties of the cross-examiner.[37] As he says, Cicero furnishes an instance of this consideration for the feelings of others in his own person, in his defense of Cluentius, one of the charges against whom was that of having poisoned a son of one of the witnesses.[38]

Turning to Cox, it is rightly said by him that the way to discredit the testimony of a witness is by closely inquiring into the SOURCES OF HIS KNOWLEDGE.[39] And here analytical skill and an intimate acquaintance with the mind and its operations is demanded on the part of the advocate.[40]

It is obvious that the advocate should not put the question directly to a witness if he is certain that the fact is as he has stated it. The witness will only be more positive since no witness will ever admit that he could have been mistaken.[41]

---

[37] *Op. cit.* 146-147.

[38] *Op. cit.* 147. Cicero referring to this charge says:
"'I deny that this young man, who you said died immediately after drinking from the cup, died on that day at all. It is a great and important falsehood. Look at the facts. I say that he came to the dinner unwell, and, with the imprudence of youth, indulged too much at it; that he was ill for some days after, and so died. Who is the witness that speaks to this? he who mourns for his death, - his father; his father, I say, who from his parental distress, would rise from the place where he is sitting to witness against Cluentius if he had the slightest suspicion of his guilt; he by his testimony acquits him. But (addressing the father) stand up, I pray, a moment, while, however painful it may be, you repeat this necessary evidence, in the course of which I will not detain you long; you have acted most righteously in not suffering your sorrow to favor a false charge against a man who is innocent.'" (*Op. cit.* 147)

[39] *Op. cit.* 397.

[40] *Ibid.*

[41] *Ibid.*

As Cox indicates, this is shown remarkably in cases where PERSONAL IDENTITY is in question.[42]

Ballantine says[43] that he has succeeded by cross-examination in cases where claims were made for injuries received in railway accidents, in showing that the claimant had not even been present at the time of the occurrence. He then refers to a case tried before the Lord Chief Justice where he assisted in exposing a very gross fraud of this nature attempted by a medical man. No witnesses were called by the company which Ballantine represented, and upon his cross-examination, supplemented by some important questions by the judge, the jury upon the plaintiff's evidence alone found a verdict for the defendants.

Returning to Cox, instead, as he says, of asking the witness whether he might not be mistaken, the advocate should proceed at once to discover the PROBABILITIES OF MISTAKE, by tracing the SOURCES OF KNOWLEDGE, and by eliciting all the CIRCUMSTANCES, internal and external, under which it was formed.[44] And he remarkably concludes this point:

> It is in this operation that the faculties of the great Advocate are displayed; this it is that calls into play his acquaintance with mental physiology, his experience of men and things, and in which he exhibits his infinite

[42] *Ibid.* Cox observes that "[e]verybody admits that there is nothing upon which all persons are so often mistaken; yet is there nothing upon which witnesses are more positive, and that positiveness is continually influencing inconsiderate juries to erroneous verdicts, as the records of our criminal law painfully prove; for, of the wrongful convictions, full one-half have been cases of mistaken identity; in which witnesses have been too positive, and juries too confiding, in a manner which their own daily experience should satisfy them to be of all others the most dubious and unsatisfactory." (p. 397).
[43] *Some Experiences of a Barrister's Life,* vol. I., London, 1882, 129.
[44] *Op. cit.* 398.

superiority over the imperfectly-educated and the inexperienced.[45]

HOW TO SHOW WITNESS IS MISTAKEN

Subsequently, Cox tries to describe the process by which the advocate can discharge this difficult duty and achieve the triumph of his art:

> The witness had detailed an occurrence at a certain time and place, and it is your purpose to show that he was mistaken in some of the particulars, and that the inferences he drew from them were incorrect, or not justified by the facts. Your first proceeding, to this end, is to *REALISE THE SCENE* in your mind. YOUR FANCY MUST PAINT FOR YOU A PICTURE OF THE PLACE, THE PERSONS, THE ACCESSORIES. You can ask the witness to repeat his story – you note its congruity or otherwise with the circumstances that accompanied it; you detect IMPROBABILITIES or IMPOSSIBILITIES. You see as *he* saw, and you learn in what particulars he saw imperfectly, and how he formed too hasty conclusions; how prejudice may have influenced him, how things dimly seen were by the imagination transformed into other things in his memory.[46]

All the above are repeated by Hardwicke,[47] who also observes that it is sometimes necessary for the advocate to show that certain facts deposed to by witnesses are impossible or at least improbable.[48]

---

[45] *Ibid.*
[46] *Ibid.* My capitals but not my italics.
[47] *Op. cit.* 161-162, 179.
[48] *Op. cit.* 160.

Cox then remarks how erring the senses are, how much their impressions are afterwards moulded by the mind and how very fallible is information. And he gives this example:

> If you make inquiry as to an occurrence in the next street, ten minutes after it has happened, and from half-a-dozen actual spectators of it, you will receive so many different accounts of its details, and yet each one positive as to the truth of his own narrative, and the error of his neighbor's. It is so with *all* testimony; and hence whatever depends upon the senses or the memory of a witness, however honest and truth-speaking he may be in intention, is fairly open to doubt, to question, to investigation, and to denial, for the purpose of showing that it ought not to be relied upon, and that it may have, upon the question under consideration, a bearing altogether different from that for which it was employed by the party who had adduced it.[49]

Hardwicke agrees that we all know how erring the senses are and how unreliable and frail human memory is. He says that it was said that Sir Walter Raleigh tore up the manuscript of the second volume of his *History of the World,* because he was unable to ascertain the true cause of a fight which took place under his own observation, beneath the window of his room in the tower where he was imprisoned, remarking that, if he could not obtain an accurate account of such an occurrence, it must be impossible to give a correct narrative of events which occurred in ages long past and in remote quarters of the globe.[50]

Subsequently, Hardwicke, dealing with a similar topic, makes this very instructive point:

> Where honest witnesses make conflicting statements, and it is necessary to ascertain which of them has sworn

---

[49] *Op. cit.* 399.
[50] *Op. cit.* 162.

truly, much depends upon the powers of perception and memory of the witnesses, and upon their ability to narrate correctly the events which they witnessed, for in order to give a true account of what he has seen, a witness MUST HAVE CORRECT PERCEPTION OF WHAT HE SAW, and a memory which is *retentive enough* to enable him to *recall* with *accuracy* all that passed in his presence. The line of demarcation between imagination and memory, however is hard to draw, and it is unquestionably true that witnesses testify to things they imagine have occurred, but which in fact have had no existence. The memory is deceitful and unreliable, and the things which are stored away in it receive color from existing impressions and experiences; the new things are mingled with the old. A writer of ability says upon this matter: 'Men have seen a very simple fact; gradually when it is distant, in thinking of it, they interpret it, amplify it, provide it with details, and these imaginary details become incorporated with the details and seem themselves to be recollections. An instance is related to Ram of witnesses in a trial in Scotland, who were unable to separate what they had read in a newspaper from what they had heard from the parties. The experienced cross-examiner, therefore, will not take the statements of honest witnesses for granted, but will investigate them thoroughly, and endeavor to show that they are mistaken as to what they think they heard or saw, and will in the mildest and most patient manner prove, by his examination of a witness who believes that he is telling the truth, that from the surrounding circumstances and the testimony of the other witnesses as well as from the unreasonableness of his story that his evidence cannot be relied upon.'[51]

---

[51] Hardwicke, *op. cit.* 162-163.

TO DISCOVER THE SOURCE OF A WITNESS'S MISTAKE

Cox clarifies that it is not enough for the advocate to ascertain that the witness is *mistaken*. He must show also whence the mistake arose. Then he says the advocate may procure this from the witness's mouth by confessing it,[52] or may show it at his address to the Jury, having ascertained to his satisfaction the mistakes of the witness and the facts which prove them to be mistakes. The second method has far better results than the first. If the advocate follows the former method the witness, having his veracity impugned, might close his mind against the advocate and resist further investigation.[53]

Ballantine states that in his time cross-examination had become more important than ever in sifting the evidence of professional witnesses in personal injury cases in which the most eminent professional men <u>occasionally fall into grave errors</u>.[54]

Hardwicke notes that the ability to cross-examine professional expert witnesses well is rare.[55] He also notes that the only safe way for an advocate who has an expert to deal with upon cross-examination, "is to hold him down to the issues involved and not allow him to cover too much ground; and above all not to argue the case of the party who has called his services into requisition".[56] In his view, the best

---

[52] "Sometimes you may procure this from the witness's mouth, thus:-Having gathered from his description that, in the circumstances of place, or time, or otherwise, as the case may be, it was impossible or improbable that he could have seen or heard enough to justify his positive conclusion, you may plainly put to him the question, how it is that, being so situated, he *could* have so seen or heard?" (*Op. cit.* 399).

[53] *Op. cit.* 399-400.

[54] *Some Experiences of a Barrister's Life,* vol. I., London, 1882, 129.

[55] *The Art of Winning Cases or Modern Advocacy,* New York – Albany, 1894, 174.

[56] *Op. cit.* 175.

method of examining expert witnesses "is to take advantage
of their enthusiasm in the cause of the party whose side they
are to maintain, and quietly and gradually lead them to an
extreme position which can neither be fortified [n]or
successfully defended."[57] He also maintains that in order that
the advocate may accomplish his purpose he must conceal his
object, and remain master of himself no matter how trying his
situation may prove. As he also claims, the advocate "must,
then, when he has led the witness to make statements which
are improbable and unreasonable, ask him to explain his
glaring inaccuracies, and if he attempts to equivocate or give
evasive evidence sternly hold him to the issues involved."[58]
As he then indicates, "in this way many experts are
completely broken down and their testimony is rendered
worthless to the side for which they are called."[59] Hardwicke
also asserts "that it is not wise to object to a witness testifying
as an expert upon the ground of incompetency, if he should
happen to be technically qualified; for jurors often being self-
made *men* are sometimes sensitive upon this point".[60] Lastly,
Hardwicke concludes that "if the testimony of an expert
witness is not to be shaken, it is better to examine him upon a
few unimportant matters, to show the jury you are not afraid
to question him and then dismiss him."[61] With all respect to
Hardwicke, my view is that in such cases it is better not to
cross-examine the expert witnesses at all.

---

[57] *Ibid.*
[58] *Op. cit.* 176.
[59] *Ibid.*
[60] *Ibid.*
[61] *Ibid.*

WHEN THE WITNESS IS LYING

Here we shall deal with false witnesses. Cox says that the art of cross-examination is not limited to the detection of mistakes but also of lies of the witnesses. In such cases, for the advocate to treat the witness as a liar he must be assured in his mind that the witness is lying.[62]

Then Cox answers a question which has often occurred to cross-examining advocates, as to whether it is more prudent for the advocate to show such a witness that he suspects him, or to conceal his doubts of his honesty. He says that either course has its advantages and its disadvantages. [63] Specifically he says this:

> (i) By displaying his doubts the advocate incurs the "risk of putting" the witness "upon his guard", "and leading him to be more positive in his assertions, and more circumspect in his answer".[64] On the other hand, as he says, "a conscious liar is almost always a moral coward; when he sees that he is detected, he can rarely muster courage to do more than reiterate his assertion, he has not presence of mind to carry out the story by ingenious invention of details and a consistent narrative of accidental circumstances connected with it."[65]

> (ii) A conscious concealment of the advocate's suspicions possesses the advantage of enabling him "to conduct him into a labyrinth" before he is aware of his design, and "so to expose his falsehood by self-contradictions and absurdities."[66]

---

[62] *Op. cit.* 400.
[63] *Op. cit.* 401.
[64] *Ibid.*
[65] *Ibid.*
[66] *Ibid.*

These two courses are also examined by Hardwicke.[67]

Cox advises that either course might be adopted, according to the CHARACTER OF THE WITNESS. He makes this distinction:

> If he is a cool, clever fellow, it may be more prudent to conceal from him your doubts of his veracity, until he has furnished you with *proofs*. If he is one of that numerous class who merely get up a story, to which they doggedly adhere, it may be wise to awe him at once, by notice that you do not believe him, and that you do not intend to spare him. We have often seen such a witness surrender at discretion on the first intimation of such an ordeal. This is one of the arts of Advocacy which CANNOT BE TAUGHT BY ANYTHING BUT EXPERIENCE". "It is to be learned only by the LANGUAGE OF THE EYE, the COUNTENANCE, the TONES OF THE VOICE, that

---

[67] *The Art of Winning Cases or Modern Advocacy,* New York and Albany, 1894, 156-:157

"In conducting the examination of a witness who he believes was sworn falsely the advocate has two courses open to him. He may show his distrust of the witness by his manner, look and tone of voice, or he may examine him as if he thought him an honest witness. We shall give further on particular directions for the guidance of the advocate in the following plan. Both courses have their advantages. The advocate, by letting the witness see that he believes he is not telling the truth, and treating him with great severity, will usually cause the witness to show his guilt by his looks, for as a general rule a liar is a moral coward. But if the witness thinks that what he has already said has been believed, he becomes careless, and if given plenty of rope he will hang himself, and the advocate can easily point out the inconsistencies in, and unreasonableness of, his testimony, to the jury in his address. When the witness has contradicted himself the advocate should not ask him to explain, but should take advantage of the contradictions in his argument to the jury. If asked to explain the witness will usually find some satisfactory explanation, even if he is obliged to invent it, take back what he said, or modify or change it."

betray to the practiced observer what is passing through the mind within.[68]

He continues "[b]ut having, AFTER A GLANCE AT YOUR MAN, resolved upon your course, pursue it resolutely. Be not deterred by finding your attacks parried at first. PERSEVERE until you have attained your object ...."[69]

From the above two passages it is clear how important it is for the advocate to understand the character of the witness and to be able to read his body language. It is important also for the cross-examiner to PERSEVERE until he has attained his object. In Cox's treatise a whole chapter is devoted to the "Will and Courage",[70] of the advocate. The secret of Napoleon Bonaparte was his strong will:

> I have succeeded in whatever I have undertaken because I have willed it. I have never hesitated, which has given me an advantage over the rest of mankind.

Elsewhere in his notable treatise, Cox explains the method of deciding whether a witness is truthful or a liar. Referring again to the important advantages of body language, he states:

> A stern, determined fixing of your eye upon his will certainly help you to assure yourself whether your suspicions are just or unjust. It may be stated, as a general rule, that a witness who is lying WILL NOT LOOK YOU BOLDY AND FULLY IN THE FACE, WITH A STEADY GAZE; HIS EYE QUIVERS AND TURNS AWAY, IS CAST DOWN, OR WANDERS RESTLESSLY ABOUT. On the contrary, the witness who is speaking the truth, or what *he believes* to be the truth, WILL MEET YOUR GAZE, HOWEVER TIMIDLY,

---

[68] *Op. cit.* 401-402. My capitals but not my italics.
[69] *Op. cit.* 402. My emphasis.
[70] *Op. cit.* chapter VII, 43-47.

WILL LOOK AT YOU WHEN HE ANSWERS YOUR QUESTIONS, AND WILL LET YOU LOOK INTO HIS EYES. There may be rare exceptions to this rule, but we can scarcely recall an instance in which it has failed to inform the Advocate whether the person he is subjecting to cross-examination is the witness of truth or of falsehood.[71]

METHOD OF SURPRISE

We shall now deal with the course of concealing from the witness the advocate's doubts. In such a case Cox says that the advocate must be a good actor. More specifically he says that if the advocate determines to adopt this course, he must be very careful "NOT TO BETRAY THEM BY HIS FACE, nor by THE TONE OF HIS VOICE, where the feeling is so often shown, while the words are otherwise framed."[72]

Hardwicke notices that "[i]n questioning witnesses upon cross-examination, advocates will find it a good plan to ask the important questions as if they were the most unimportant, and in fact to appear to the witness to want exactly the opposite of what he really wants to get out of them."[73] He notices also that this course is often pursued by some of the most successful lawyers.

On the same topic, Cox emphasizes:

> To be a good Advocate you MUST BE A GOOD ACTOR, and it is one of the faculties of an actor to command his countenance. <u>Open gently, mildly; do not *appear*</u> <u>to doubt him</u>; go at once to the marrow of the story he has told, as you were not afraid of it; make him repeat it; then carry him away to some distant and collateral topic,

---

[71] *Op. cit.* 405-406. My capitals, my underline but not my italics.
[72] *Ibid.*
[73] *The Art of Winning Cases or Modern Advocacy,* New York and Albany, 1894, 176-177.

and try his memory upon *that,* so as to divert his thoughts from the main object of your inquiry, and prevent his seeing the connection between the tale he has told and the questions you are about to put to him. Then, by slow approaches, bring him back to the main circumstances, by the investigation of which it is your purpose to show the falsity of the story.

The design of this manœuvre is, of course to prevent him from seeing the connection between his own story and your examination, so that he may not draw upon his imagination for explanations consistent with his original evidence; your purpose being to elicit inconsistency and contradictions between the story itself and other circumstances, from which it may be concluded that all or a great part of it is a fabrication.[74]

Subsequently, Cox gives[75] an instance of this sort of examination which fell within his own experience. It is very useful to refer to this example here.

In an affiliation case, the mother had sworn distinctly and positively to the person of the father, and to the time and place of their acquaintance, fixed, as usual, at precisely the proper period before the birth of the child.

The time sworn was the middle of May and the place the putative father's garden. For an hour the mother endured a strict cross-examination but she was not to be shaken in any material part of her story. Her cross-examination proceeded as follows:

> *Q.* You say you walked in the garden with Mr. M.?
> *A.* Yes.
> *Q.* Before your connection with him?
> *A.* Yes.
> *Q.* More than once;
> *A.* Yes; several times.

---

[74] *Op. cit.* 402-403. My underline.
[75] *Op. cit.* 403-404.

Q. Did you do so afterwards?
A. No.
Q. Is there fruit in the garden?
A. Yes.
Q. I suppose you were not allowed to pick any?
A. Oh! yes; he used to give me some.
Q. What fruit?
A. Currants and raspberries.
Q. Ripe?
A. Yes?

This was enough as the mother was detected at once. The alleged intercourse was in the middle of May. However, currants and raspberries are not ripe till June. In this case the mother's whole story was not true. Cox remarks that "[s]he had fallen in with the suggestion about fruit, to strengthen, as she thought, her account of the garden; but she did not perceive the drift of the questions, and consequently had not sufficient self-command to reflect that fruit is not ripe in May."[76]

This is a good illustration of the manner in which the most acute witness may be detected in a lie. Cox advises "that PATIENCE in the pursuit is always necessary".[77] In his illuminating words which follow:

> You may be baffled again and again, but be careful never to let it be seen that you are baffled. Glide quietly into another track, and try another approach; you can scarcely fail of success at last.[78]

And then follows a profound saying: "NO *FALSE* WITNESS IS ARMED AT *ALL* POINTS."[79]

---

[76] *Op. cit.* 404.
[77] *Ibid.* My emphasis.
[78] *Ibid.*
[79] *Ibid.* My capitals but not my italics.

What happens now when the Judge does not see the drift of the cross-examiner,[80] especially if he is young, and complains of tediousness or repetition.[81] According to Cox the cross-examiner in such a case must firmly but respectfully assert his right to conduct his examination after his own fashion and proceed unperturbed in his path.[82] He says also that the duty of the advocate is to his client and he must discharge it FEARLESSLY.[83] After a while the Judge will discover that the cross-examiner does not act without a sufficient reason and that he has a design in his cross-examination.[84]

On the point under discussion, Ballantine gives an instance from his own experience:

> An experienced equity judge once said to me in relation to a question I had asked, 'Really, this is a long way from the point.' 'I am aware of that, my lord,' was my answer. 'If I were to begin any nearer, the witness would discover my object.'[85]

---

[80] As Cox says, it must be confessed that cross-examination is often conducted at random, without aim, or plan, or purpose so that Judges may well be excused for complaining. (*op. cit.* 405).

[81] On this issue Hardwicke says the following: "The benefits of cross-examination are sometimes defeated by the interposition of the court, to require an explanation of the motive and object of the questions proposed, or to pronounce a judgment upon their immateriality: whereas experience frequently shows that it is only by an indirect, and apparently irrelevant inquiry, that a witness can be brought to divulge the truth which he prepared himself to conceal; the explanation of the motives and tendency of the question furnishes the witness with a caution that may wholly defeat the object of it, which might have been successfully attained if the gradual progress from immateriality to materiality was withheld from his observation...." (*The Art of Winning Cases or Modern Advocacy,* New York and Albany, 1894, 236-237).

[82] *Op. cit.* 404-405.

[83] *Op. cit.* 405.

[84] *Ibid.*

[85] *Some Experiences of a Barrister's Life,* vol. I, London, 1882, 127.

METHOD OF BOLD AND OPEN ATTACK

Then Cox deals with the case where the cross-examiner decides to adopt the OTHER COURSE, i.e. to bring the falsehood out of the witness by a bold and open attack.

When the advocate decides to pursue his plan of bold attack, "there needs to be no circumlocution, no gradual approaching".[86] He must go straightaway to his object. He must make him repeat it slowly. It may happen that under the discompose of the advocate's detection of his purpose, he will directly vary from his former statement.[87] If he does so in material points, which are sufficient to discredit him, "it will usually be the most prudent course to leave him there, self-condemned, instead of continuing the examination, lest you should give him time to rally, and, perhaps, to contrive a story that will explain away his contradictions."[88] Cox then notes that if the witness is well learned and repeats the narrative very closely as at first, the cross-examiner will have to try another course.[89]

Subsequently, Cox explains in detail one course he is suggesting:

> Procure from him in detail, and let *his words* be taken down, the particulars of his story, and then QUESTION HIM AS TO ASSOCIATED CIRCUMSTANCES, upon which he is not likely to have prepared himself.... Having obtained his answers, permit to him no pause, but instantly take him to a new subject; lead his thoughts away altogether from the matter of your main topic. The more IRRELEVANT your queries the better; your purpose is to occupy his mind with a new train of ideas. Conduct him with DIFFERENT PLACES AND PERSONS AND

---

[86] *Op. cit.* 406.
[87] *Ibid.*
[88] *Ibid.*
[89] *Ibid.*

EVENTS. Then as SUDDENLY, in the midst of your questionings, when his mind is the MOST REMOTE FROM THE SUBJECT, when he is expecting the next question to the one that has gone before, *SUDDENLY* return to your FIRST POINT, not repeating the *main* story (for this, having been well learned, will probably be repeated as before), BUT TO THOSE CIRCUMSTANCES ASSOCIATED WITH IT UPON WHICH YOU HAD SURPRISED HIM INTO *INVENTION* ON THE MOMENT. It is most probable that, after such a diversion of his thoughts, he will have forgotten what his answers were, what were the fictions with which he had filled up the accessories of his false narrative, and having no leisure allowed to him for reflection, he will now give a different account of the circumstances, and so betray his falsehood.[90]

And then follows a great advice as to the above method: "OF ALL THE ARTS OF CROSS-EXAMINATION, THERE IS NONE SO EFFICIENT AS THIS FOR THE DETECTION OF A LIE."[91]

Cox reverts to this technique later in his treatise and explains it in even more detail. He says that the advocate must try the witness by questions on matters which only bear INDIRECTLY upon the point in issue.[92] For example, if the witness has sworn that on a certain day a person made to him a certain statement, the cross-examiner cannot directly shake the fact thus sworn to, for the witness has but to adhere to his assertion and will baffle any amount of direct interrogation.[93] However, as Cox continues, it is not at all likely that the witness "has prepared himself WITH ALL THE

---

[90] *Op. cit.* 406-407. My capitals but not my italics.
[91] *Op. cit.* 407. My capitals.
[92] *Op. cit.* 430.
[93] *Ibid.*

ACCOMPANYING PARTICULARS".[94] Cox then gives
samples of questions to be asked by the cross-examiner:

> Where was the conversation held?
> At what time of the day?
> Who was present?
> Were they sitting or standing?
> How did he come to the place?
> Whom did he meet on the way?
> How was he dressed – and the other party?
> Did they speak loud or low?
> Did they eat or drink together, and what?
> Did anybody come in while they were talking?
> How long were they together?
> When they parted which way did each take?
> Whom did he meet afterwards?
> At what time did he reach his home?
> And so forth, as the particular circumstances of the case
> may suggest, but always, if possible, preferring facts
> spoken BY OTHER WITNESSES, so that you may expose
> him, not only by his contradictions, but by the
> TESTIMONY OF OTHERS.[95]

Hardwicke also alleges that the cross-examiner should
conduct the cross-examination with the testimony of other
witnesses in view, and endeavour, if, possible, to secure a
contradiction by the witness under examination, of the other
witnesses on whose side he has been called.[96] The story of
Susannah and the Elders in the Apocrypha affords an
admirable example. The two false witnesses were examined
out of the hearing of each other, and on being asked under

---

[94] *Ibid.* My emphasis.
[95] *Ibid.* My emphasis.
[96] *The Art of Winning Cases or Modern Advocacy,* New York and Albany,
1894, 160.

what sort of tree the criminal act was done, the first said a "mastick tree", the other a "holm tree."[97]

Another example given by Hardwicke[98] is from Bentham's[99] *Rationale of Judicial Evidence* where the following is stated: "To the merits of the cause, the contents of the supper were altogether irrelevant and indifferent. But if, in speaking of a supper given on an important or recent occasion, six persons, all supposed to be present, give a different bill of fare; and contrariety affords evidence pretty satisfactory (though but of a the circumstantial kind) that at least some of them were not there." According to Hardwicke, the most usual application of this rule is in detection of fabricated alibis. These seldom succeed if the witnesses are skilfully cross-examined out of the hearing of each other; especially as courts and juries are aware that a false alibi is a favourite defense with guilty persons, and consequently listen with suspicion even to a true one.[100]

Cox further observes that when questions of this kind are RAPIDLY PUT they deprive the false witness of the opportunity to fit them to his previous story. He also gives instructive advice to lawyers:

> You should also carefully AVOID PUTTING them in any NATURAL SEQUENCE OF TIME OR PLACE, for that is to suggest to him a story which he will invent quite as rapidly as you can construct your questions. DISLOCATE THEM as much as possible. TAKE NOW ONE PART OF THE STORY, THEN ANOTHER. DODGE HIM BACKWARDS AND FORWARDS, from one object to the other, so that it shall be impossible for him to be prepared by one question FOR THE NEXT, or

---

[97] *Ibid.*
[98] *Op. cit.* 160-161.
[99] Bentham, *Rationale of Judicial Evidence, Specially Applied to English Practice,* London, 1827, Colorado, 1995, vol. 2, p.9.
[100] *Op. cit.* 161.

that one answer shall be the prompter of its successor. The difficulty of doing this well is very great, and therefore, perhaps, it is that it is so rarely seen to be well done....[101]

Another excellent plan, Cox suggests, is to take the witness through his story, "BUT NOT IN THE SAME ORDER OF INCIDENTS IN WHICH HE TOLD IT."[102] He explains this in more detail, thus:

> Dislocate his train of ideas, and you put him out; you disturb his memory of this lesson. Thus, begin your cross-examination AT THE MIDDLE of his narrative, then jump to one end, then to some other part THE MOST REMOTE from the subject of the previous question. If he is telling the truth, this will not confuse him, because he speaks from impressions of mind; but if he is lying, he will be perplexed and will betray himself, for, speaking from the memory only, which acts by association, you disturb that association, and his invention breaks down.[103]

Apart from the above two excellent plans, Cox recommends this process of detection when the cross-examiner is satisfied that the witness is drawing upon his invention: RAPID FIRE OF QUESTIONS. He clarifies that the cross-examiner must give "NO PAUSE" to the witness between the questions, "NO BREATHING PLACE", "NO TIME TO RALLY".[104] Elsewhere in the same notable work he says that the advocate must give to the witness "no time for reflection and so engaging his attention that he shall not have leisure to digest his answers, or to see how they square with the story he has already told."[105]

---

[101] *Op. cit.* 431. My emphasis.
[102] *Ibid.* My capitals.
[103] *Op. cit.* 407-408. My emphasis.
[104] *Op. cit.* 408. My emphasis.
[105] *Op. cit.* 429.

As he clarifies, "[f]ew minds are sufficiently self-possessed as, under such a catechising, to maintain a consistent story. If there be a pause or a hesitation in the answer, you thereby lay bare the falsehood. The witness is conscious that he dares not stop to think whether the answer he is about to give will be consistent with the answers already given, and he is betrayed by his contradictions."[106] In this process, Cox states, it is necessary to fix him to TIME, and PLACE and NAMES.[107] He then gives some samples of questions:

> "You heard him say so?"
> "When?"
> "Where?"
> "Who was present?"
> "Name them."
> "Name one of them."[108]

As he explains, names, times and places are not readily invented, or, if invented, not readily remembered.[109] If the tale be true, the answers to such questions present themselves instantaneously to the witness's lips.[110] Cox concludes this point thus:

> They [the answers] are so associated in his mind with the main fact to which he is speaking, that it is impossible to recall the one without the other. Collateral circumstances may be forgotten by the most truthful or even be unobserved; but TIME, PLACE and AUDIENCE, are PART OF THE TRANSACTION, without which memory of the fact itself can scarcely exist.[111]

---

[106] *Ibid.*
[107] *Ibid.*
[108] *Ibid.*
[109] *Ibid.*
[110] *Op. cit.* 409.
[111] *Ibid.* My emphasis.

Elsewhere in his notable treatise, Cox explains this method in more detail:

> The principle of this manner of cross-examination is, that *TRUTH IS ALWAYS CONSISTENT WITH ITSELF*. If the witness is telling the truth, his answers will be in *substantial* accordance with the story he has already told, and with any questions that may be put to him. He has no need to consider their BEARING, and therefore his reply is as prompt as memory. On the contrary, the witness who is telling a false story cannot so construct it that it shall be consistent – not merely in itself, for that is not difficult – but with other ASSOCIATED CIRCUMSTANCES which it is impossible to anticipate.[112]

Similarly Hardwicke observes that it is very important for the witness to be examined rapidly so that he can have no time to concoct plausible answers between the questions. If the witness is honest, he will answer the questions without hesitation but if he is swearing falsely, by this method his detection will nearly always follow.[113]

According to Cox, another useful method of attacking the witness who is lying is this:

> Without previous questioning, come at once to the point, and ask him to repeat his account of the transaction. He will do so in almost the selfsame words, with the same aspect and manner, and in the same tone, differing palpably from his bearing and tone and language before and after the episode. So certain is this test that, if it fails, you may fairly give to the witness the benefit of the doubt, and say that, whatever other objections may be offered to

[112] *Op. cit.* 429-430. My capitals but not my italics.
[113] *The Art of Winning Cases or Modern Advocacy,* New York and Albany, 1894, 156.

his testimony, it is not a story learned and repeated by rote.[114]

Elsewhere in his work, Cox says that there is but one method of defeating falsehood in the witness-box. That is by involving it <u>in a maze of contradictions which it is almost impossible for the most skilful liar to avoid</u>. That is so because the quickest mind cannot in a moment calculate the effect of its present answer upon the past, or anticipate the bearing of the reply it is about to give upon the questions that are to follow[115]. He concludes with a remarkable saying:

HENCE IT IS THAT CROSS-EXAMINATION HAS BEEN ALWAYS DEEMED THE SUREST TEST OF TRUTH, AND A BETTER SECURITY THAN THE OATH.[116]

On the treatment of dishonest witnesses, Hardwicke says that he disagrees with Archbishop Whately and alleges that a sudden, bold and unexpected question does many times surprise a witness and lay him open. The mind of a witness must be diverted from the part of his testimony where it is hoped to make him speak the truth, until the proper moment.[117]

---

[114] *Op. cit.* 420. See also section on body language pp. 35-44 *ante.*
[115] *Op. cit.* 428.
[116] *Ibid.* My capitals.
[117] *The Art of Winning Cases or Modern Advocacy,* New York and Albany, 1894, 149.

WEIGHT TO BE GIVEN TO VARIATIONS
AND DISCREPANCIES IN TESTIMONY

Cox admits that there is no branch of cross-examination on which a wider difference of opinion prevails than upon the weight to be given to VARIATIONS by a witness in the telling of a story.[118] Advocates, he explains, usually dwell upon them as evidence of falsehood, while Judges almost always direct the Jury that they are rather evidence of honesty.[119] Cox then endeavours to reconcile these two views, by using his knowledge of psychology, as follows:

Memory is association: ideas return linked together as they were originally presented to the mind, and the presence of one summons the others by suggestion. An event is witnessed, and the scene and its accessories are impressed upon the mind. But they are only impressed there *as the spectator beheld them*, and not necessarily as they were in reality. It is necessary to ascertain also *the medium* through which he saw or heard, before we can properly estimate the value of his memory. When called upon to bear testimony of fact, if a man desires to tell the truth, he will describe, as nearly as he can in words, so much as he can recall of the circumstances. But it by no means follows that, every time he recalls the scene, it should present itself to his mind in precisely the same aspect; and for this reason: the mind does not revive the whole at once, but in succession, and some portions of it will come back more vividly at one time than at another, and, by their very vividness, recall other associations before unremembered. Hence, *differences* in description, and especially new circumstances introduced into a repeated narrative, although each repetition should *vary* from all the former ones, by the addition of some things

---

[118] *Op. cit.* 409.
[119] *Ibid.*

and the omission of others, <u>do not afford the slightest grounds for imputing perjury to a witness</u>. On the contrary, they are rather a presumption in his favour, for an invention that is learned would probably be recalled *as it was learned,* with the same facts, and almost in the same words.[120]

However, it is otherwise with DISCREPANCIES of statement. As Cox says "[t]hese cannot exist in a truthful narrative".[121] He also clarifies that "[r]epeated ever so frequently, and whatever the *variance* in detail, the STORY WILL ALWAYS BE CONSISTENT WITH ITSELF, and with its former assertions."[122] A positive discrepancy is proof that the witness is not speaking the truth.[123]

---

[120] *Op. cit.* 419-410. My underline but not my italics. In his Study *The Psychology of Memory and Recollection,* Paper of the Psychological Society of Great Britain, No. 9, London, 1876, Cox distinguishes "memory" from "recollection" as follows:
"*Memory* and *Recollection* are not only taken as synonymous terms, but the two processes are almost universally assumed to be the same. They are in fact two wholly different processes. *Memory* is the faculty by which the impressions made upon the brain are retained either by the brain itself or by something receiving the impressions made upon the brain. *Recollection* is the process by which these impressions are recalled. *Memory,* as suggested above, is probably a Psychic process. *Recollection* is usually, perhaps not always, a brain process." (*op. cit.* 7). Elsewhere in the same Study he says: "It is not the *Memory* that is good or bad but the capacity for *Recollection.* This is proved by abundant experience. The act of storing in the memory is performed at one time, and the act of reproducing those stores is performed at another and later time, and often after intervals of many years." (*op. cit.* 8-9). Cox also makes this very instructive point about "memory" and "recollection": "...the capacities of Memory so much vary, not only in various persons, but in the same individual.... The same person often possesses an extraordinary memory of facts and none for words; another can remember words accurately, but not music, and so forth. So it is with Recollection..." (*op. cit.* 11).
[121] *Op. cit.* 410.
[122] *Ibid.* My capitals but not my italics.
[123] *Op. cit.* 411.

Cox's wise and fair theory is that the advocate has no right to attempt to discredit a witness by perplexing him into contradictions unless he entertains the strongest suspicion that he is not telling the truth.[124] Next he says that if the advocate reasonably suspects that the story is forged, or coloured, or only partially told, it will be his duty to discover and display its defects. If he believes it to be falsehood or a misrepresentation, it will be his endeavour to make the witness contradict himself. Lastly, if he believes that there is a *suppressio veri,* his ingenuity will be exerted to extract the truth that had been withheld.[125]

UNIMPORTANT DISCREPANCIES

Immediately after-wards, Cox comes with a significant warning as to the weight the advocate must give to SMALL and UNIMPORTANT DISCREPANCIES of a witness. His extremely useful warning is this:

> Beware that you fall not into the fault, only too common with the inexperienced, of seizing with eager triumph upon *small* and *unimportant* discrepancies. Every man's experience teaches him that there are few who can tell the same story twice in precisely the same way, but they will add or omit something, and even vary in the description of minute particulars. Indeed, so well known is this, that a *verbatim* recital of the same tale by a witness is usually taken as satisfactory proof that he is repeating a lesson he has learned, and not narrating facts he has seen. To be of any value to you for the purpose of discrediting his testimony the contradiction must be on some material particular, or some incidents connected with it which, according to common experience, a man is not likely to

---

[124] *Op. cit.* 415.
[125] *Op. cit.* 416.

have observed so slightly that, in the course of ten minutes, he would give two different descriptions of it. In this, as in all matters of an Advocate's duty, remember that you are dealing with a Jury composed of men of common sense and experience of life, who cannot understand refined distinctions, and have no respect for petty artifices and small triumphs over a witness's self-possession or memory, and that you will not win their verdict unless by your cross-examination you show that the witness is not *puzzled,* but lying.[126]

Hardwicke says that it is cruel, brutal and impolitic for a lawyer to examine a witness upon the theory that he is swearing falsely when he believes that he is only mistaken as to certain immaterial matters in his testimony.[127]

As we have seen, Cox says that repetition of questions should be avoided unless it is used as a means for the advocate to detect the falsity of the witness.[128]

WITNESS' LACK OF MEMORY

Cox also examines the case where the witness chooses not to answer saying that he does not remember, though the advocate is aware that he could tell him a great deal, if he pleased, but has reasons for forgetting. To conquer such a witness, Cox says, the advocate needs as much patience as art.

He set outs three rules: "The first rule is to keep your temper; the second, to be as resolute as himself; the third, to

---

[126] *Op. cit.* 416-417. My underline.
[127] *The Art of Winning Cases or Modern Advocacy,* New York and Albany, 1894, 156.
[128] See pp. 55-57 *ante.*

discover his weak place: every person *has* some weak point, through which he is accessible."[129]

Subsequently, he explains these rules: If the advocate betrays the slightest want of temper, the witness will have the advantage of him for he will enlist his pride in defence of his determination. If he shows him that he is resolved to have an answer, he will shake him "by the influence which the strong Will always obtains over the weaker one and by that wonderful power which PERSISTENCY NEVER FAILS TO EXERCISE".[130] Lastly, to find out his weaknesses, the advocate must "PERUSE HIS CHARACTER" by the art which, it is assumed, he has cultivated – *"THE ART OF READING THE MIND IN THE FACE"*.[131]

According to Cox, the surest method to make the witness speak is to be SMILING AND JOCOSE.[132] If this method fails, Cox suggests another method. The advocate must procure from the witness an admission of so much THAT HE CANNOT HELP TELLING THE WHOLE.[133] Cox then explains in detail this method:

> The difficulty of this consists in the extreme caution required to approach him, so that your object shall not be perceptible; so to frame your questions that he <u>shall not see the connection between the answer he is about to give</u> and <u>the confession you desire to extract from him.</u> In appearance, the questions must be dissevered from the immediate subject sought, but, in fact, they must be associated with it. THE APPROACH MUST BE SO GRADUALLY MADE AS NOT TO EXCITE SUSPICION; and perhaps <u>it is well to open with something quite foreign to the subject-matter.</u> Having

---

[129] *Op. cit.* 413.
[130] *Op. cit.* 414. My emphasis.
[131] *Op. cit.* 414. My capitals but not my italics.
[132] *Ibid.*
[133] *Ibid.*

obtained an answer, you put another query that appears naturally to follow from the former, and so on until you link with the question something that is associated with the matter sought for. It is not easy for a witness to discover THE LINKS OF SUCH A CHAIN, and he is sure to make some admissions that negative his alleged ignorance of the transaction, and compel him, having yielded so much to surrender the whole.[134]

Hardwicke also deals with the case where the witness says that he does not remember. In that case, he says, the cross-examiner may exhaust his ingenuity and may try every artifice of which he is master to make him remember.[135]

WITNESS VOLUNTEERING TESTIMONY

Cox alleges that it is wrong to suppose that when a witness dispenses with questions and pours out his whole story in a continuous stream, he is therefore always lying.[136] We have dealt with this point in the section dealing with body language and there is no need to repeat what has been said there. The advocate's care will be to distinguish between the witness who runs through his story telling the truth, or merely repeating a lesson learned by heart (taught testimony).[137] As he observes, "close observation" will enable him "to discover a difference in the look, the tone, the manner and the language".[138] Again, therefore, BODY LANGUAGE is important. More details on this topic were given in the section

---

[134] *Op. cit.* 414-415. My underline and my capitals.
[135] *The Art of Winning Cases or Modern Advocacy,* New York and Albany, 1894, 152.
[136] *Op. cit.* 417.
[137] *Op. cit.* 418.
[138] *Ibid.* My underline.

on BODY LANGUAGE[139] and there is no need to repeat them here.

Cox also deals with the case of the witness who is biased by his feelings and interest. Such a witness must be approached, according to Cox, in another fashion. He says the following: Direct questions will not suffice and the advocate must approach the witness with caution and indirectly. He must begin by giving him credit for good intentions. He must not appear to mistrust him. He must flatter him even with the assurance that he believes he desires to tell the whole truth. As Cox says, it is a great point to have the witness well pleased with himself for the advocate's purpose is not only to unveil him to others but to strip from his own eyes the veil of SELF-DECEPTION, so that his vanity will be enlisted against the advocate. The advocate must start by conciliating him and reminding him by his first question that he is a party to the cause and has the strongest interest in the result. Next he will assure him of his own confidence that, in spite of this bias, he desires to tell the whole truth and that although he has no intent to deceive, the truth is not as he has stated, blinded by his feelings or his interest.[140]

According to him, the advocate's duty is either to elicit the very truth as it was or to show that, being thus self-deceived, the witness's testimony is not to be relied upon.[141] The advocate must remember the position of the witness. The witness "has *impressions* upon his mind which he *believes* to be *true*. He, therefore, unhesitatingly swears to them as *facts*."[142] Cox rightly considers that "it is obvious that direct questioning will fail to disturb them, for to a mere repetition of the question as to what he saw or heard, the same answer

---

[139] See pp. 35-44 *ante.*
[140] *Op. cit.* 424-425.
[141] *Op. cit.* 425.
[142] *Ibid.*

as before will be as promptly and distinctly given."[143] He then clarifies that "[t]he only means, then, of shaking such testimony is to show it <u>to be inconsistent</u> WITH OTHER FACTS, or with those STRONG PROBABILITIES arising out of the usual order of things, the ready perception of which constitutes what is called *common sense.*"[144]

Lastly, Cox makes it clear that there is no difference in this respect in the cross-examination of a witness having the interest of a party, and that of a witness biased by any other interest. The process will be the same as to all such. The advocate must approach the witness by INDIRECT AND NOT BY DIRECT questions, and employ all his efforts to elicit contradictions and inconsistencies between the facts positively asserted by the witness and other undoubted facts, or between his testimony and probability and common sense.[145]

On the handling of witnesses who are interested in the settlement of the case, Hardwicke has this to say:

> In the examination of witnesses the advocate must not lose sight of the fact that the interest of the witness in the subject-matter of the controversy, if he is a party to the cause, or interested in the settlement of a question which arises in the case, or if he is related by consanguinity or affinity to the party in whose favor he has been called, or is at enmity with the party against whom he is testifying, or the friend or enemy of either of the parties, will be apt to color his story, and make it favorable or unfavorable according to the interest or bias of the witness. And this is often true when the witness is honest. By exaggeration, evasion, equivocation, indistinctness or pretended want of memory, a witness may do great damage to the side which he is called to assist. If the advocate is as familiar with all the facts of the case as he should be, he can usually take

---

[143] *Ibid.*
[144] *Ibid.* My underline, my capitals but not by italics.
[145] *Op. cit.* 426.

advantage of these things by showing that their testimony does not agree with the facts as deposed to by the other witnesses.[146]

FACTS OCCURRING IN PRESENCE OF WITNESS ONLY

Lastly, Cox deals with a kind of testimony which will sometimes battle the advocate's utmost skill, and discusses it so that the advocate may be prepared for it when it comes, lest it should throw him into an awkward perplexity:

> It is the case of a witness who swears positively to some single fact, occurring when no other person was present, or but one now dead or far distant, and whom, therefore, it is impossible to contradict, and equally difficult to involve in self-contradiction because all the circumstances may be true, except the one which he has been called to prove.[147]

To make this more intelligible, Cox gives the following example:

> In order to prove a link in the chain of a pedigree, a witness swears to a conversation with one of the family now dead, in which an ancestor of the claimant was alleged to have been recognized as a relative. It is very probable that the witness did at some time hold some conversation with the deceased in the manner and place described. He has only *added to it* the one false assertion that such a statement was made. Now it is obvious that in this case all the usual methods of detecting falsehood will fail. The witness can neither be contradicted, nor will he contradict himself, for all that he has told is true, save a few added

---

[146] *The Art of Winning Cases or Modern Advocacy,* New York, Albany, 1894, 161.
[147] *Op. cit.* 431-432. My underline.

words, and you will not shake him by an examination as to the circumstances, for they also would be truly stated.[148]

Cox indicates that the advocate's difficulty in this case is great for any protracted cross-examination of such a witness may show him to the Jury to be perfectly truthful in all other parts of his story. His advice is for the advocate <u>to appeal to the Jury to look with suspicion upon evidence so easily forged and so impossible to be disproved</u>.[149] He should also ask the Jury to try the worth of such evidence by its intrinsic probabilities, showing them if he can how improbable it is that such statement should have been so made, or such a circumstance have occurred.[150]

Ballantine alleges[151] that a truthful witness usually adheres to the dry statement of facts, and avoids diverting attention by introducing irrelevant matter. He says that he thinks a remark once made by him to the Jury upon the following occasion is a sound one:

> It was upon a trial before Chief Justice Erle. I had put a question to a witness as to what he was doing at a particular time, this being a matter important to the inquiry. 'I was talking to a lady' was his answer; adding, 'I will tell you who she was, if you like. You know her very well.' I made no observation at the time, but when addressing the jury said that my experience led me to the conclusion that honest witnesses endeavoured to keep themselves to the facts they came to prove, but that lying ones endeavoured to distract the attention by introducing something irrelevant; and I think this remark is worth consideration, and points out one of the tests of truth or falsehood in a person under examination.

---

[148] *Op. cit.* 432. My underline but not by italics.
[149] *Op. cit.* 432-433. My underline.
[150] *Op. cit.* 433.
[151] *Some Experiences of a Barrister's Life,* vol. I, London, 1882, 126.

Some judges upon the bench never shone in this branch
of advocacy, and scarcely appreciate the value of it, and a
refinement that now attends trials, and contrasts in many
respects favourably with the coarseness of a former period,
occasionally interferes with the force and persistence
required in dealing with some persons in the box.[152]

Hardwicke considers that Curran's method of dealing
with untruthful or unwilling witnesses was often very
effective, and refers to it as described by Phillips:

At cross-examination, the most difficult, and by far the
most hazardous part of a barrister's profession, he (Curran)
was quite inimitable. There was no plan which he did not
detect, no web which he did not disentangle, and the
unfortunate wretch, who commenced with all the
confidence of preconcerted perjury, never failed to retreat
before him, in all the confusion of exposure. Indeed it was
almost impossible for the guilty to offer a successful
resistance. He argued, he cajoled, he ridiculed, he
mimicked, he played off the various artillery of his talent
upon the witness; he would affect earnestness upon trifles,
and levity upon subjects of the most serious import, until at
length he succeeded in creating a security that was fatal, or
a sullenness that produced all the consequences of
prevarication. No matter how unfair the topic, he never
failed to avail himself of it; acting upon the principle that,
in law as well as war, every stratagem was admissible. If
he was hard pressed, there was no peculiarity of person, no
singularity of name, no electricity of profession, at which
he would not grasp, trying to confound the self-possession
of the witness by the, no matter how excited, ridicule of
audience.[153]

---

[152] *Op. cit.* 126-127.
[153] *The Art of Winning Cases or Modern Advocacy,* New York and
Albany, 1894, 151.

Though Hardwicke rightly does not approve of the unfairness of which Curran's biographer admits that he was guilty, there is much to be learned, as he says, by an attentive consideration of the great advocate's method as related.[154]

Remember

- *The cross-examiner must follow the principles of morality when conducting a cross-examination. He must behave as a "Christian gentleman".*
- *The cross-examiner has no right to attempt to discredit a witness by perplexing him into contradictions, unless he entertains the strongest suspicion that he is not telling the truth.*
- *The approach of the cross-examiner should be dependent on whether the witness is mistaken or is lying.*
- *If the witness is mistaken, the cross-examiner must begin with conciliation by removing the fear of the witness. He must proceed very gently until he sees the witness reassured. He must inquire into the sources of his knowledge in order to discover the probabilities of a mistake.*
- *If the witness is lying, the cross-examiner must use the method of surprise or the method of bold attack depending on the character of the witness.*
- *In using the method of surprise the advocate must act like a good actor. He must prevent the witness from seeing the connection between his own story and the purpose of cross-examination. He must gently and mildly without appearing to doubt the witness elicit inconsistency and contradictions between his story and other circumstances from which it may be concluded that all or part of his evidence is a fabrication.*

---

[154] *Op. cit.* 151-152.

• In using the method of bold and open attack, the advocate must not gradually approach the witness but must go directly to his object. If the witness is well-taught and repeats his story, the cross-examiner must indirectly question him on associated circumstances. He may also take the witness through his story but not in the same order of incidents in which he told it. Another good technique is the rapid fire of questions so that the witness does not have time for reflection. He must involve him in a maze of contradictions which it is almost impossible for the most skilful liar to avoid.

• The cross-examiner must realize the difference between variations in the story and discrepancies as to material facts. Despite the latter, the former is not evidence of falsehood.

• In a case where the witness chooses not to answer saying that he does not remember, the cross-examiner must use the smiling method and should frame his questions in such a way that the witness will not see the connection between the answer he is about to give and the confession the advocate desires to extract from him.

• In the case of a witness who is biased by his feelings and interest, the best way is to approach him with caution and indirectly. The cross-examiner must begin by conciliating him and must then go on to shake his testimony by showing it to be inconsistent with other facts or with strong probabilities.

• Lastly, when a witness swears positively to some single fact, occurring when no other person was present, or except one now dead or far distant, and it is obvious that all the usual methods of detecting falsehood will fail, the cross-examiner must appeal to the Jury to look with suspicion upon evidence so easily forged and so impossible to disprove.

RUFUS CHOATE
THE MODEL

RUFUS CHOATE WAS A MODEL CROSS-EXAMINER

Rufus Choate is referred to by Hardwicke as a model cross-examiner who combined all the qualifications and abilities an excellent cross-examiner should have.[1] Hardwicke says that Daniel Webster considered Rufus Choate as a marvel.[2] And he observes that Webster's opinion of Choate, who was one of his dearest friends, was the unanimous opinion of those of his professional brethren who knew him intimately. Hardwicke refers with approval to one of Choate's biographers, without however naming him. This biographer[3] says of Choate:

> But his cross-examination was a model. As was said, in speaking of his conversations, he never assaulted a witness as if determined to brow-beat him. He commented to me once on the cross-examination of a certain eminent counsellor at our Bar with decided disapprobation. Said he: 'This man goes at a witness in such a way that he inevitably gets the jury all on the side of the witness. I do not,' he added, 'think that is a good plan.' His own plan was far more wary, intelligent and circumspect. He had a profound knowledge of human nature, of the springs of human action, of the thoughts of human hearts. To get at these and make them patent to the jury, he would ask only a few telling questions – a very few questions – but generally every one of them was fired point-blank and hit the mark. He has told me, 'Never cross-examine any more than is absolutely necessary. If you don't break your witness, he breaks you; for he only repeats over in stronger language to the jury his story. Thus you only give him a second chance to tell his story to them, and besides, by some random question you may draw out something damaging to your own case.' This last is a frightful liability.

---

[1] *The Art of Winning Cases or Modern Advocacy,* New York – Albany, 1894, 180.
[2] *Ibid.*
[3] I found out that his biographer was Edward G. Barker and the said quotation is taken from his book *Reminiscences of Rufus Choate – the Great American Advocate,* New York, 1860, 153-154.

Except in occasional cases, <u>his cross-examinations were as short</u> as his arguments were long. <u>He treated every man who appeared like a fair and honest person on the stand, as if upon the presumption that he was a gentleman;</u> and if a man appeared badly, he demolished him; <u>but with the air of a surgeon performing a disagreeable amputation – as if he was profoundly sorry for the necessity.</u> Few men, good or bad, ever cherished any resentment against Choate for his cross-examination of them. His whole style of address to the occupants of the witness stand <u>was soothing, kind and reassuring.</u> When he came down heavily to crush a witness, <u>it was with a calm, resolute decision, but no asperity – nothing curt, nothing tart.</u>[4]

Choate's method of cross-examination may be instructive to every lawyer. All the principles we have discussed in this book were followed by Choate and in the above passage we can see many of them underlined by the present writer.

Remember

- *Rufus Choate was the wizard of cross-examination who combined all the qualifications and abilities an excellent cross-examiner should have.*

---

[4] *Op. cit.* 180-181. My underlining but not my italics.

www.ingramcontent.com/pod-product-compliance
Lightning Source LLC
Chambersburg PA
CBHW021713210326
41599CB00013B/1638